EDEN PRESS

Monographs in
Women's Studies

Series Editor:
Sherri Clarkson

# A NEW MYTHOS

The Novel of the Artist as Heroine 1877-1977

**Grace Stewart**

© **Eden Press Women's Publications, Inc. 1979**

Published by:
Eden Press Women's Publications, Inc.
Box 51, St. Alban's, Vermont 05478 U.S.A.
*and*
Eden Press Women's Publications,
1538 Sherbrooke St. West, #201, Montreal, Quebec, Canada H3G 1L5


ISBN 0-88831-030-7
Library of Congress Catalog Card Number 78-74840

Dépôt légal - primière trimestre 1979
Bibliothèque nationale du Québec


Typeset in Century Textbook, 10 point on 12, by
Vicky Bach, Hamilton

Printed in Brattleboro, Vermont, U.S.A.

# CONTENTS

# PREFACE

This work stems from an interest in the myths used in literature, the images of women found there, and the burdens a woman writer might feel while operating within a tradition of such myths, especially those pertaining to the artist. By examining how female writers structure their novels of the artist as heroine and therein treat certain existing myths and mythic images, I conclude that the mythic pattern of the female artist differs significantly from the so-called universal pattern.

In order to limit the variables, this study deals only with novels written in English by American, Canadian, and British women and only with those novels whose heroines have worked seriously toward an expressed or obvious goal of becoming an artist, whether the art form be concrete (as in painting) or ephemeral (as in acting). To indicate the constancy of the pattern, I examine works written in different eras, that is, between 1877 and 1977.

Although I do not investigate the origins of myth, I do list the various schools of thought concerning them, since critics may question woman's capacity for myth-making or insist on her automatic inclusion in the collective unconscious. A brief look at the prevalent arguments provides a perspective which allows, if not an open mind, at least an overview of alternatives. Therefore, as background, Chapter I reviews theories pertinent to the origins of myth, to the myths artists have favored for self-portrayal, to the possible psychological bases for their choices, and to the *Künstlerroman*, where those mythic patterns and images often appear.

Chapter II shows how women, in their novels of the artist as heroine, have used one patriarchal myth, Goethe's *Faust,* or reacted to ideas implicitly and explicitly expressed therein. In this study, Goethe's version of *Faust* represents patriarchal myths in general and myths of the artist in particular for several reasons. First, it depicts women in roles traditionally assigned to them in myths--as beauteous but distressed damsels, as inspirations leading to spiritual realms, as awesome mothers, and as frightening monsters or witches. Second, *Faust* polarizes, among other themes, several that are important to the artist, who is notoriously an overreacher and a divided being. Third, Goethe's version of the Faust legend is most frequently mentioned in the *Künstlerromanen* examined. Fourth, his version, if not the best, is the best-known of the works based on the Faust legend.

Chapter II having dealt with the psychological and sociological burdens of female novelists operating in the tradition of a patriarchal myth, Chapter III focuses on what might be called a matrifocal myth. The powers that ultimately rule the universe are still masculine, but the concerns and issues are feminine. Used as an overlay in Chapter III, the matrifocal myth of Demeter/Persephone synthesizes elements common to mothers and daughters and highlights a common strand in the *Künstlerromanen* written by women.

In Chapter IV the journeys to the interior--taken in most of the novels considered--receive individual attention. The study reveals striking parallels of structure and of imagery pertaining to this journey.

As a whole, Chapters I through IV move from the general to the specific and from the abstract to the concrete in their focus on problems of the individual female artist. The conclusion attempts to synthesize and to suggest research for the future.

For my own research, I am indebted to several organizations and individuals. The Wayne State University fellowships awarded 1972-73 and 1976-77 provided valuable time away from my teaching commitments. Members of the Grosse Pointe Chapter of the American Association of University Women heard parts of Chapter III; an all-male audience of the Michigan Academy of Science, Arts, and Letters listened to parts of Chapter II. Comments from these segregated audiences stimulated new ideas and prompted refinement of old ones.

I especially thank Dr. Joanne V. Creighton, E. M. Broner, and Dr. Jacqueline Zeff for information about ongoing research, for constructive criticism, and for the encouragement each offered. Among other friends, Dr. Doranne Crable-Sundmacher, Dr. Gladys Garner Leithauser, and Ms. Norma Merry provided sustenance, each in her own way. I also acknowledge a debt to Ms. Patty Lynam, an independent businesswoman and a superb typist. My insights evolved not only from literary sources but from the personal experiences of these and other women--relatives, friends, and colleagues.

To

Rachel Harriet Stewart

and

Marshall Stewart

## Chapter I

# BACKGROUND: MYTH, THE ARTIST, AND THE KÜNSTLERROMAN

*"Misbirth is possible from the mythological womb as well as from the physiological...."* [1]

Joseph Campbell

*Myth:* The word evokes the mysterious, calls forth images of serpents and wild swans, glorifies the mundane, predicates the primitive, or suggests the sublime. Word magicians have for centuries used mythic images consciously or unconsciously to structure, expand, crystallize, cloud, or clarify their writings. To discuss these images is to soar toward illumination in the mode of Icarus or to plunge into an abyss. A Western critic who focuses on myth must be prepared not only to discuss but possibly to take a fall, for she must battle with giants from several realms: anthropology, psychology, sociology, biology, theology, and feminology. Each has representative hordes--functionalists, Euhemerists, structuralists, Freudians, Jungians, and diffusionists.

The source of myths is one of the focal points of dispute. To explain the existence of similar mythic images in different times, places, and cultures, the diffusionists posit that myths originated in one locality and then spread to the rest of the world. Scholars favoring a theory of convergence suggest that human beings, subject to similar stresses, respond with similar dreams, wishes, or artistic impulses. Functionalists search for ways in which a myth arises to fill the need of a society or to suit the purpose of its leaders. Psychologists debate the universal source of mythic images--the id, the anima, the mother/child relationship, or the dominance of one side of the brain. Theologians and idealists argue the existence of an absolute which reveals itself through the human mind. Structuralists research myths serially in "gross constituent units"[2] to unearth the "basic logical processes which are at the root of mythical thought."[3] In all of these fields, feminologists re-examine the experience of women, for feminists argue that most previous research has been biased by a patriarchal if not a male perspective and that, as a result, the terms "universal" and "basic" may apply neither to the source of the myths nor to the myths themselves. Without becoming mired in any one of these sciences, the literary critic is faced with the necessity of coping with, if not using, their theories and their jargon. If I must pledge allegiance to one of these disciplines, I admit a bias of the woman's perspective.

Having shown my colors, I might set the boundaries for this quest by defining the terms "myth" and "mythic images." According to the Follett edition of *The Classic Greek Dictionary* (1962), *mythos* means a "story, a *poetic* or *legendary tale,* as opposed to the *historical* account." Some people might therefore call it art. However, Lévi-Strauss argues that myth is language, but of a distinct kind, not to be criticized as art: "Myth always refers to events alleged to have taken place in time: before the world was created, or during its first stages. . . . . But what gives the myth an operative value is that the specific pattern described is everlasting; it explains the present and the past as well as the future."[4] For someone who is asserting the eternal existence of logical processes in the human mind, his definition is suitable. Malinowski calls myth "a narrative resurrection of a primeval reality."[5] For someone who views myth as a primitive, prelogical explanation of the phenomena, that definition helps to reinforce his position. Joseph Campbell defines myth as "a revelation of transcendental mysteries."[6] Since he believes that nature is a determinant and that "the myth is a group dream projected from the personal-collective vision of a seer: a gifted individual,"[7] Campbell formulates a definition that excludes the possibility of a myth's originating solely in the social sphere. In direct opposition, the historical or Euhemeristic definition suggests that myths deify or glorify great mortals or important events.

Proponents of a wide variety of perspectives agree that myths focus on crucial periods in human life or evolution: cosmological explanations, parent/child relationships, the individuation of the self, sexual explorations, incest, rape, chaos, war. The degree of truth in these myths is debatable. Elizabeth Janeway describes them as "both true and false, false in fact, but true to human yearnings and human fears and thus, at all times, a powerful shaping force."[8] If one believes myths to be "prescription"[9] rather than description, the definition of mythic statements as distortion of reality or mere wishful thinking undermines their effectiveness.

It would seem, then, that to define terms is to reveal one's bias. Part of the difficulty lies in the nature of the term, *myth,* when used in a general way. It has come to mean many things, depending on the predilection of the user. As Wallace Douglas so cleverly writes, "The word is protean and its fate is procrustean . . . ."[10] Despite this difficulty, Alan Watts has formulated one definition that is not too restrictive: "Myth is to be defined as a complex of stories--some no doubt fact, and some fantasy--which, for various reasons, human beings regard as demonstrations of the inner meaning of the universe and of human life."[11] This definition contains enough for the transcendental, the psychological, the sociological, and the literary interpretation.

When Watts's definition is used as a base, "mythic images" can be defined as "concrete expressions evoking a sensory experience of the inner meaning of the universe and of human life." To appreciate the scope of such concrete expressions, Joseph Campbell's *The Mythic Image* is useful. Photographs of ancient and modern sketches, paintings, and sculptures which depict similar sets of circles, mandalas, earth goddesses, lingams, omphales, fountains, wells, trees, flowers, snakes, fowl, fish, and wild beasts in various combinations indicate man's desire to permanently record the drama of truths as he or his people perceived them. Individual reproductions, though chosen from different times, various places, and distinct cultures, show remarkable similarities. Literary examples of such images abound in the Bible, in classical mythology, and in literary works. Mythic images and patterns are repeated in many legends of the saints (e.g., St. George and the Dragon) and of sinners (e.g., Dr. Faustus). Artists have employed these images and patterns to create great works of art like *Faust.* The transformation of myths continues.

Campbell believes that this continuation of the imagery and poetic insights of myth depends on the artist. He writes, "As far as I know, in the myths themselves the origins of their symbols and cults have always been attributed to individual visionaries--dreamers, shamans, spiritual heroes, prophets, and divine incarnations." 12 Campbell may be right. When one thinks of the visions of Buddha, Christ, and the prophets of the Old Testament, the outpourings of "dreamers" like Blake and Yeats, and the prehistoric drawings in the caves which depict an occasional shaman among the beautiful abstractions of animals, the evidence seems to confirm the visionary as the transmitter of myths, if not the originator.

However, if critics reject Campbell's somewhat vague theories of the origin of myth in favor of theories asserting a higher, transcendental power, or a description of natural events like the movement of the sun and seasons, 13 or a psychologically-based drive (logical, pre-logical, or illogical), the following facts remain:

1) Myths and mythic images, whether believed or merely desired as potential, would not have been transmitted through different cultures, times, and conditions, unless propelled by some powerful agent (whether the power was in the hands of the elite--the wealthy, the noble, the printers--or in the hands of the masses--via intensely-held beliefs, revolutionary spirit, or purchasing power).

2) Myths have held literary ground in this expanding universe despite the overriding sway of rational, scientific, logical thinking in the twentieth century. Some modern writers like Eliot, Joyce, and Lowell have voiced the necessity of myths as connectives in an otherwise atomistic, relativistic world.

3) Myths are often outpourings of crucial periods in life or history. Wheelwright claims: "Every change of human condition--birth, puberty, initiation, betrothal, marriage, pregnancy, paternity, specialization of occupation, death--is mythopoeically regarded as a passage from a state of self that is dying to a state of self newly born." 14 Frye has described the Western mythical pattern as that of creation, fall, exile, redemption, and restoration, 15 a form which reaffirms man's control over death--symbolically as in a new personality or actually as in the Christian belief in resurrection and the immortality of the soul.

4) Myths and mythic images evoking this pattern are articulated or transmitted by those who have imagistic power and sensitivity. Because the artist becomes acutely aware of his status in relation to the external world, he often depicts the process of this discovery in terms of birth-death-rebirth. The self is depicted sometimes as dying, leaving its

surroundings, and being reborn as a separate entity; at other times as dying, leaving its individual state to be reborn through nature or love as a transcendent being in tune with the universe. Both processes involve the creation or re-creation of the self.

Otto Rank noticed this tendency of the artist and described it in 1914 as "The Myth of the Birth of the Hero." Examining the sagas of Moses, Oedipus, Paris, Perseus, Romulus, Tristan, Gilgamesh, Hercules, and Jesus, Rank noted a series of uniformly common features:

> *The standard saga itself may be formulated according to the following outline: The hero is the child of most distinguished parents, usually the son of a king. His origin is preceded by difficulties, such as continence, or prolonged barrenness, or secret intercourse of the parents due to external prohibition or obstacles. During or before the pregnancy, there is a prophecy, in the form of a dream or oracle, cautioning against his birth, and usually threatening danger to the father (or his representative). As a rule, he is surrendered to the water, in a box. He is then saved by animals, or by lowly people (shepherds), and is suckled by a female animal or by an humble woman. After he has grown up, he finds his distinguished parents, in a highly versatile fashion. He takes his revenge on his father, on the one hand, and is acknowledged, on the other. Finally he achieves rank and honors.* [16]

Rank's assumption is that such myths are created by adults who are repressing or remembering their own infantile fantasies. He argues that even if the historical theory is sound and that myths are descriptions of actual heroes and events, the repetitive pattern of myths, legends, and sagas in several different times, for various cultures, and under different conditions suggests that the people who tell or retell the tale align the series of events to resemble their own fantasies. In a similar way, those behavioralists who argue that the sufferings and struggles of the potential hero might actually condition him and cause his "hero personality" must once again account for the repeated transmission of the tales as fulfilling some need of the powerful. Rank, of course, insisted on the dream of the masses as explaining both the

5

source of myth and its repeated transmission, and he furthermore believed that most of the myths contained a significant feature found in the Lohengrin saga, which he analyzed in detail. In his studies, Rank confirmed Freud's interpretation of the pattern: "The cyclic character of the Lohengrin saga is referred . . . to the *fantasy of being one's own son* . . . ." [17] To Rank, this fantasy explains the universal nature of the origin and appeal of the patterned myth.

In describing the same mythic pattern, Jung sidestepped the sexual or Oedipal complications when he interpreted these heroic actions as "the portrayal of the human libido and its typical vicissitudes" and the cyclic pattern "as the fantasy of being born again." [18] Feminists may react negatively to many of Jung's theories, but this explanation of the mythic pattern is in its scope less sexist, more "universal" than Rank's. The fantasy may explain the appeal of art which employs this structure. Frye claims that, whereas the mediocre work of art does not contain a center which attracts readers, "the profound masterpiece draws us to a point at which we seem to see an enormous number of converging patterns of significance." [19] Myth and mythic structure evoke this sensation.

Critical focus has shifted away from myth as history, as ritual, as natural outpourings inherent in all men, or as a gift from the Absolute, whether it be God, a demiurge or the Muse. Despite Lévi-Strauss's insistence that myth, unlike art, is believed and therefore not subject to criticism, critics continue to examine myth as art, perhaps because modern artists include myth or mythic images and allusions in their works. Their use of myths may be considered "consummatory," Wheelwright's category for products of "a somewhat late and sophisticated state of cultural development, a post-romantic attempt to recapture the lost innocence of the primitive mythopoeic attitude . . . ." [20]

Specific myths seem to be more attractive than others to the artist when he is writing autobiographically. Ernst Kris has described the typical "legend of the artist": Because his status personality is similar to but removed from the common man, the artist creates a "family romance" and identifies with heroes, specifically divine or demonic beings. Some favorites of the artist include myths of Prometheus, Daedalus, Faust, and Icarus. Kris has documented incidents of "enacted biography" that show the tendency of artists not only to identify in fiction with these heroes but also to follow in their own lives the traditional mythology of the artist. [21]

Because the *Künstlerroman* deals with the development, formation, or special problems of the artist, such mythological patterns or images appear frequently in these works. The most typical and perhaps best-known example of the *Künstlerroman* is Joyce's *Portrait of the Artist as a Young Man,* which is admittedly autobiographical and which obviously depends on mythology. The hero, Stephen Dedalus, identifies not only with the mythical Daedalus but also with Christ. In Thomas Mann's *Doktor Faustus,* Adrian Leverkühn exemplifies the artist who identifies with demonic powers. Both are twentieth-century novels, and both contain the mythic pattern of a quest.

The journey or quest is an important element in myth, in fiction, and in life. Erich Heller has written a series of essays which, all together, give an historical overview of man's pattern of quest. In particular, the story of Faustus in its several stages (Gent's, Marlowe's, Goethe's, and Mann's, for example) reveals the changing historical attitudes toward the search for knowledge and the changing focus from the outer to the inner world. Erich Heller claims that a passion for understanding lured nineteenth-century minds "toward the rational conquest of the human world only in order to prove to them its absolute meaninglessness." [22] This quest led to another--to the "world of human inwardness"--the only reality in an atomistic universe. Heller identifies the pilgrim of this journey as a Faustian figure, "a Don Juan of the Mind," [23] chasing the ideal.

According to Gerald Jay Goldberg, the quest, so important in other genres, is especially prominent in the *Künstlerroman.* In this fiction, the journey involves a creative process in more ways than one. In the twentieth-century *Künstlerroman,* particularly, he claims, "The theme of the quest for identity is intimately connected with the concept of the discovery of self through the process of creation so that the actual creation of a work has become the subject of many contemporary artist-novels." [24]

Thus, the writer of the *Künstlerroman,* searching for the artist's beginnings, struggling to understand himself, and trying to create something with meaning, follows the pattern of modern man's search for existence in a meaningless universe. The quest is topical, yet universal, for the pattern repeats the search for the honeyed land, the holy grail, the lifted maya, the rebirth of the soul, nirvana, or the womb. Frye goes so far as to claim that the central myth in most narrative literature is the quest-myth. [25] Rank and Jung believe that artists try to recapture the spirit of childhood, when freedom and innocence accompanied security and nourishing love given by the parents--a golden age. That attempt to recapture paradise lost is repeated in mythic patterns and images of the quest.

Campbell describes this monomythic pattern as "a separation from the world, a penetration to some source of power, and a life-enhancing return." [26] Whether it be the action of Buddha, Christ, Moses, Prometheus, Aeneas, or the artist, myths proclaim that "the really creative acts are those deriving from some sort of dying to the world." [27] Campbell in this statement means "creative" in a concrete way. The positive result of the quest is the "elixir" with which the hero returns--a message or a gift of eternal life, laws to live by, fire, knowledge, or a work of art. The hero returns, in this universal pattern, with self-salvation or a gift for society or both. The question arises: Is this myth really universal? It seems pervasive.

When we turn from psychological, archetypal, or literary patterns to specific responses in specific situations, a different pattern seems to emerge. In studying such responses in a cultural situation, Ralph Linton finds variances clustered around specific statuses: "In practically all cases, different response configurations are characteristic for men and for women, for adolescent and for adults, and so on." [28] With this study in mind, Kris worked out the special "status personality" of the artist, [29] as previously described. This personality can easily assume mythic proportions. Other notables, like Rank and Campbell, have argued that this identification of the artist with mythic figures and with recurring patterns in mythology manifests the "universal" urge or wish. But the authors who created these works and the critics who theorized about the universality of their patterns were all male.

In developing his idea of the artist's distinct "status personality," Kris ignored Linton's claim that, as groups, men and women *respond differently* to cultural situations. If Linton's theory is valid (and Kris's theories depend on its being valid), is it not possible that they respond differently to myths? Can these myths then be considered universal, or are they constructs of a patriarchal culture that reinforces its wishful thinking by creating or responding positively to these fantasies? Indeed, is the mythic pattern of the artist as hero a universal one? Does the mythic pattern of the artist as heroine differ?

Partial answers to these questions can be found in the *Künstler-romanen* written by women, novels critically ignored as a group, perhaps due to their different focus. Both males and females use personal experiences as bases for their works. Since the feminine realm is limited in scope as defined by males, females have not been able to write so comprehensively as Joyce or Homer or Goethe about their experiences in wars, sailing vessels, universities, brothels, or pubs. Even though some women, like Mme. de Staël and George Sand, have managed to break social barriers and to draw upon the larger scope of their experience, their novels of the artist as heroine rarely receive particular notice in the tradition of the *Künstlerroman*.

In one of those rare instances, Maurice Beebe claims that *Corinne* belongs to a group of "guidebooks to the art capitals of Europe presented in the guise of sentimental romances." [30] Asserting, nevertheless, that this "art novel" served as a model for the genre, Beebe emphasizes the similarities to the patriarchal form and ignores differences that place the work in a distinct category of *Künstlerromanen* written by women. Similarly, he remarks that *Consuelo* is "one of the founders of the Bohemian tradition in artist fiction" [31] but neglects to mention that a woman may have to depict her heroine as Bohemian in order to vault convention.

Although these novels, written in foreign languages, are not a part of this study, they are reminders that the focus here is the novel of the artist as heroine and that further discussion about myth in general is obviously inconclusive without data on women's responses to and uses of myths and mythic patterns. The casual statement about vaulting conventions contains a kernel of what follows in this examination of *Künstlerromanen* written by and about women operating under the psychological and sociological burdens of a patriarchal society and its myths.

9

Subsequent chapters, dealing with novels of the artist as heroine, will reveal how a number of female novelists treat the Faust myth or its inherent patriarchal aims and ideas, what specific issues or experiences inform the *Künstlerromanen* written by and about women, and how the female's journey to the interior and the mythic images used therein differ in some ways from the so-called universal pattern.

## Chapter II

## FAUST AND THE ARTIST AS HEROINE

*"Human discernment*
*Here is passed by;*
*Woman Eternal*
*Draw us on high."* [1]
  Final lines in Goethe's *Faust,* 1831

*"Women can't be writers. They don't know blood*
*and guts and puking in the streets and fucking whores*
*and swaggering through Pigalle at 5 A.M. . . ."*[2]
  Notes from a lecture at Barnard, 1961

### BACKGROUND

Faust, in the medieval book-lined tower, typifies the being who longs for mutually-exclusive goals. Frustrated by such longing, he exclaims:

*Two souls, alas, are dwelling in my breast,*
*And either would be severed from its brother;*
*The one holds fast with joyous earthy lust*
*Onto the world of man with organs clinging;*
*The other soars impassioned from the dust,*
*To realms of lofty forebears winging.* [3]

This exclamation could come from the lips of most artists, divided as they are by the need to create and the need to live. Faust's twin goals might be called "The Ivory Tower" and "The Sacred Fount," labels which Maurice Beebe has given to the resting places of artists clinging to the two traditions of art:

> *The man seeks personal fulfillment in experience, while the artist-self desires freedom from the demands of life. . . . The Sacred Fount tradition tends to equate art with experience and assumes that the true artist is one who lives not less, but more fully and intensely than others. . . . The Ivory Tower tradition, on the other hand, exalts art above life and insists that the artist can make use of life only if he stands aloof . . . .* 4

Although the male artist feels divided by his separate needs, both involve action--gaining experience or knowledge, or creating a work of art. Faust epitomizes the man of action, and Goethe's drama glorifies the spirit of striving, particularly as that spirit is embodied in the male.

In *Faust*, men strive restlessly, search incessantly for knowledge, experience lust, lust for experience, attempt Byronic ascents toward upper realms and courageous descents to earthly or oceanic caverns, and generally become embroiled in alchemic, magical, political, economic, and literary stews. Females embody motherhood, purity, fear of experience, domesticity, selflessness, and the status quo. They are nymphs, goddesses, and witches or wenches confined to the kitchen. Despite the fact that Faust's actions are often futile and destructive, they are visionary and dynamic. By contrast, Gretchen's dutiful and domestic behavior is productive but unpraised. Goethe depicts her not as *striving* but as *being*--pure, dutiful, domestic. Although order and cleanliness pervade her domicile, the shopping, scrubbing, and polishing occur, unsung, behind the scene. Even the effective but Faust-directed poisoning of her mother takes place behind the curtain, whereas her weakness, distress, passivity, and steadfast love for Faust are staged. Likewise, Helen's beauty, the Mothers' awesome presence, and Galatea's oceanic ride on the chariot shell are states of being, not of doing. As Hans Eichner claims, the two ideals of conduct--the steadfast purity and innocence of the females and the ceaseless activity of the males--are incompatible. 5

The man who concerns himself with the plight of the Philemons and Baucises in isolated cottages around the world will not complete enormous water projects that flood such homes. A great work of art demands sacrifice from people. As Goethe writes, "Man ever errs the while he strives." [6] In order to accomplish, Faust must not be swayed by his conscience. If Euphorion had been cautious, he would not have been able to plunge so deeply into the abyss or to soar so high on his rebound. The excesses of these male characters are frequently harmful or fatal, but nevertheless dynamic and vital. By contrast, the passive, pure, and innocent seem pale, even sterile. Gretchen's disoriented refusal to join with the devil results in her death. She is not a defiant St. Joan. Helen and Galatea are ineffectual and ephemeral. Hans Eichner claims that in *Faust*, only the Virgin Mary can avoid the "harmonious mediocrity" of this world's existence and yet still act as a genuine synthesis. To him, she represents "the Eternal Feminine without this world's limitations, the symbol of a purity that, by a miracle, is not sterile." [7] The genuineness of an unearthly and immortal synthesis is questionable. However, there can be no doubt that through these female figures in general and the "eternal woman" as an abstract ideal, Goethe effects his resolution. In so doing, he follows a pattern recognizable to his audience.

Although "the assumption that normal men are naturally dominant and aggressive, while normal women are naturally submissive and masochistic"[8] is gradually being dispelled, Leon Salzman, as well as other psychologists, realizes that both men and women historically have "come to accept this notion and to actively oppose its abolition." [9] Nancy Chodorow reports on contemporary studies which "demonstrate that the socialization of boys tends to be oriented toward achievement and self-reliance and that of girls toward nurturance and responsibility. Girls are thus pressured to be involved with and connected to others, boys to deny this involvement and connection." [10] Furthermore, she notes that this sex-role distinction between *doing* and *being* is reiterated in several souces--anthropological, sociological, and psychological--and suggests that legends, myths, and fantasies reflect the need for men to establish their maleness and to externalize their dread of women--by conquering through "naming" such horrors as Medusa, by glorifying and adoring women, such as the adoration of Helen and Galatea, or by debasing them as pitiful and weak. [11] Western literature in general and *Faust* in particular both reflect and reinforce one mythic image of woman--"The Eternal Feminine."

Having to work within this tradition, the female writer is handicapped in two ways. First, she must consciously or unconsciously reject the image of woman as passive, weak, selfless, and unthinking or accept her unwomanliness if she actively and selfishly seeks experience, knowledge, and pleasure. Because, as Mary Ellmann notes, "our concept of creation is profoundly intellectual and self-directed,"[12] the procreative, other-directed, and nourishing role of woman is antithetical to the role of the artist. As the lecturer from Barnard suggests (in this chapter's epigraph), one tradition of the male artist is experiential, a seeking of personal fulfillment; the other, as Beebe suggests, is reflective, aloof, a self-centered and solitary existence. Neither tradition befits the womanly role of selfless involvement with and connection to others. Thus, the female writer must defy the cultural definition of artist or of woman if she is to remain artist and woman.

Second, she must work within the confines of a tradition which depicts beauty, inspiration, and life in female form. Goethe followed and reinforced this tradition. He synthesized "the idea in the form of a woman,"[13] and the ideal of moral purity in *das ewig Weibliche*, just as Stephen Dedalus experienced his epiphany in the form of an Irish girl straddle-legged in a stream. Readers and critics are accustomed to this tradition. As Bergstraesser writes, "The polar constitution of the universe manifests itself through organic life as a male-female polarity."[14]

If this polarity is repeatedly depicted in terms of *doing* and *being*, then Faust's divisiveness between his earthy and his spiritual nature becomes a dual dilemma for the female artist as heroine. For the female novelist, Beebe's labels of Ivory Tower and Sacred Fount have a different meaning. Women placed on ivory pedestals traditionally are consciences of society, decorative ornaments, or angelic agents to a heavenly realm. Women playing the role of fountains traditionally become Dianas of Ephesus, sources of an erotic, earthy, or hellish life; indeed, they become images of the Earth Spirit which Faust momentarily evoked. Sometimes women play both roles. For instance, Faust's Margarete and Gretchen are one and the same, both inspiration and peasant. Rather than *work* in fount or tower, the female artist is *confined* by one or the other tradition. How, where, or what can the female artist create?

14

She must choose: She may consciously or unconsciously reject this tradition of polarity or of the female form as synthesizing agent. She may write didactic feminist fiction which critics will debase as art. She may create a hero or adopt a masculine identity and remain within the tradition. She may create fictions which transmute the old or construct new myths (like those of Anaïs Nin or Monique Wittig) which prove unacceptable to readers dependent on the traditional. She may seek to erase all sexuality and establish an androgynous or asexual protagonist. When, as a female, she creates an artist as heroine, she is denied these convenient escapes. Her heroine may therefore remain disintegrated, estranged, or unsuccessful--a failure as a woman or as an artist. Seeking to unify her tortured self, the active, assertive heroine may seek wholeness through an asexual religious experience. Or, the heroine-artist may accept the traditional view of the female as supportive or inspiring and also accept the image of her artist-self as a monster or an aberration of some kind. The dilemma of the artist is doubly frustrating for a woman. These conflicts--between life and art and between the woman and the artist--usually form a vital part of the novel of the artist as heroine. An examination of several novels will reveal that the dual dilemma manifests itself in the structural pattern, in the explicit statements of the heroines, and in the imagery emphasizing the social barriers the female artist faces.

## THE BELL JAR

The very title of Sylvia Plath's novel, *The Bell Jar* (1963), metaphorically suggests a social barrier. The artist-heroine feels stifled, as though suspended in a bell jar. She admits wanting, like Faust, "two mutually exclusive things at one and the same time."[15] However, her divisiveness and eventual madness are caused not by a dualism of the earthy and spiritual Esther so much as by a stifling of the female artist-self who cannot emerge in the roles society presents her.

An ability to win scholarships and awards allows Esther to enter a glamorous world. Once there, she is given no acceptable role models. Other female award-winners play traditionally feminine roles of self-effacement and allow men to maul them. For these women, relationships with men take precedence over self-achievement. Evolving from a man-centered culture, Esther Greenwood is hemmed in by a pervasive belief: "What a man is is an arrow into the future and what a woman is is the place the arrow shoots off from" (p. 79). This place can be pictured as a setting for Helen, the passive catalyst of wars or the muse of poetry; as Gretchen's domicile, a place of serenity, order, and purity; as the cavern of the Mothers, a creative nurturing ground; or as the oceanic realm of Galatea, the source of life or eros. Esther rejects all these passive or unrewarding roles and chooses instead the restlessness of Faust: "The last thing I wanted was infinite security and to be the place an arrow shoots off from. I wanted change and excitement and to shoot off in all directions myself, like the colored arrows from a Fourth of July rocket" (p. 92).

However, she has been told so often, "a man's world is different from a woman's world and a man's emotions are different from a woman's emotions" (p. 89), that she is almost convinced marriage and motherhood represent the only fulfillment for a woman. As an active, artistic female, she has no acceptable models, only those she labels "weird old women" (p. 248) who want to adopt her in some way. She knows that the price of their care and influence is to resemble them, and she rejects both "The Eternal Feminine" and "The Poetically Masculine."

Swayed by the self-protective need to reject the roles of mother, virgin, or eternal woman to whom males return for purification or refreshment, Esther establishes her sexual identity by taking birth-control precautions and then having intercourse. Afterward, she muses: "I couldn't possibly be a virgin any more. I smiled into the dark. I felt part of a great tradition" (p. 258). With which tradition does Esther identify? With Gretchen, the shamed and betrayed woman who is seduced but who remains selfless? With the pitiful fallen women of Gretchen's village who are stoned or hanged? Or with Faust, accumulating knowledge in and for itself, the demon-driven spirit feeding on dead selves and exploited others? Since Esther's sexual experience results in a blood bath, an abortive rather than a positive or procreative experience, Plath seems to be rejecting Eros as a creative principle for women--at least, for so long as males are fitting diaphragms, lying about their own purity, or denying responsibility for their bloody deeds. When Esther sends her violator a bill, she turns her back on the Eternal Feminine and momentarily frees herself from the suffocating bell jar.

That Esther feels temporarily refreshed does not suggest a heroic return to society. Buddy, her "fiancé," wonders who will marry her

16

now that she has been labeled an asylum mate. Esther pointedly says, "And of course I didn't know who would marry me now that I'd been where I had been. I didn't know at all" (p. 272). This line is ambiguous. Esther can be refusing to admit "where she had been," insane, or she can be suggesting that as a healthy female artist, perhaps no one will marry her. If she can avoid thinking of herself as "insane," she is well aware that society will view her as abnormal in either case, as artist or ex-inmate. Even if she chooses the traditional female role she may not escape suffocation, since she envisions most women outside the asylum--the co-eds, the bridgeplayers, the gossips-- as stifled and on display, too. For Esther Greenwood, the Sacred Fount is bloody, and the Ivory Tower is suffocating. Neither tradition nourishes this female artist.

## THE SONG OF THE LARK

Trying to work within the tradition of novels dealing with the artist, Willa Cather points out in the author's preface to *The Song of the Lark* (1915) some of the similarities and differences of her book and Wilde's *The Picture of Dorian Gray*. Although her *Künstlerroman* highlights performing rather than productive creativity, both works depict division of the artist. In Cather's novel, "The harassed, susceptible human creature comes and goes, subject to colds, brokers, dressmakers, managers. But the free creature, who retains her youth and beauty and warm imagination, is kept shut up in the closet, along with scores and wigs."[16] Despite this existence in a metaphoric tower, "Her artistic life is the only one in which she is happy, or free, or even very real" (p. vi). Although Thea is described as happy, Cather's use of the phrase "is kept shut up" indicates a contradiction between personal choice and outside pressure. The polarity of solitude and companionship causes a frequent conflict in the *Künstlerroman,* but in one written by a female, the solitude is antithetical to her concept of womanhood, as well.

In growing up, Thea is expected to care for her younger brother, to appease this idol whenever necessary, to pull him on his wagon, and even to give up practice time when he's teething. She caters to her brother Thor willingly, despite the fact that she condemns such passivity in others, particularly Spanish Johnny's wife: "She was think-

17

ing that there is nothing so sad in the world as that kind of patience and resignation. It was much worse than Johnny's craziness. She even wondered whether it did not help to make Johnny crazy. People had no right to be so passive and resigned" (p. 55). This conflict between activity and passivity, between others' needs and her own, pervades her early years.

Concerned as an adolescent about a tramp who dies of neglect in Moonstone, she gets a lecture from Dr. Archie: " 'While we are in this world we have to live for the best things of this world, and those things are material and positive. Now, most religions are passive, and they tell us chiefly what we should not do' " (p. 175). Trying to instill her with his own assertiveness, he tells her: " 'The things that last are the good things. The people who forge ahead and do something, they really count' " (p. 176). Human relationships, especially concern over potential failures, cannot be "fixed" or rendered immortal. She is torn by a dual responsibility:

> She has always believed that by doing all that was
> required of her by her family, her teachers, her pupils,
> she kept that part of herself from being caught up in the
> meshes of common things. . . . It was as if she had
> an appointment to meet the rest of herself sometime,
> somewhere. (p. 272)

The responsibility she feels toward artistic perfection and that which she feels towards others must be divided. Given the opportunity to advance her career, Thea envisions her struggle in Faustian terms. Tempted by a need for peace and for her family, she reminds herself, "If she failed now, she would lose her soul" (p. 466). Thea must choose between these needs. As if to apologize for Thea's turning her back on her family, Cather writes: "There are passages in life when that fierce, stubborn self-assertion will stand its ground after the nobler feeling is overwhelmed and beaten under" (p. 274).

Thea's relationship with men must also be cut off. Her father realizes early that she is not the marrying kind: " 'She's too peppery and too fond of having her own way. Then she's always got to be ahead in everything. That kind . . . don't make good wives' " (p. 129). A man who thinks she will make him a queen is teased by fellow workers:

" 'The man that gets her will have to wear an apron and bake the pan-cakes' " (p. 141). Fellow boarders "could see no reason for keeping up with a girl who, under her jocularity, was cold, self-centered, and unimpressionable" (p. 327). A "jolly" potential lover warns her that most other jolly men "want to be the amimating force. When they are not around, they want a girl to be--extinct" (p. 393). Whereas Faust experiences earthly bliss with Helen and is saved eventually by Gretchen's intercession, men become bothersome to Thea.

Fred Ottenburg embarrasses her by marrying her without divorcing his wife. Thea rejects his wealth and the label of mistress or of "kept woman," and borrows money elsewhere to maintain her independence. She needs to remain unsullied, because her confidence in herself, her free spirit, will determine her success in music. She wants to continue "waking up every morning with the feeling that your life is your own, and your strength is your own, and your talent is your own; that you're all there, and there's no sag in you" (p. 34). Trying to remember a musical phrase in Wagner's *Ring* while walking on the street, Thea is approached by a man. She angrily cries, "O let me *alone*!" The man vanishes "like the Devil in a play" (p. 254).

She views this and other male interference as a power that is bent on taking her private ecstasy from her and barring her from her goals. Her only lover backs off complaining, " 'Loving you is an heroic discipline. It wears a man out' " (p. 559). Going beyond what Goethe calls human discernment, Gretchen and the Virgin Mary are capable of such eternal love; most men are not.

The male artists in the novel are nurtured by their women: Mrs. Tellamantez cares for Spanish Johnny, the musically-obsessed guitarist, no matter how many times he runs off or gets drunk. Mrs. Harsanyi is able to create a comfortable atmosphere for her composer-husband, no matter how poor or busy he is. Mr. Wunsch, the eccentric piano-teacher who occasionally goes on a drunken spree, is nursed and fed by Paulina Kohlers and her husband.

Years later, when she reaches her goal, Thea admits that she has had to encourage her destructive demon, creative hate: " 'A contempt that drives you through fire, makes you risk everything and lose everything, makes you a long sight better than you ever knew you could be' "

19

(p. 550). Seeing her when she has achieved success, Dr. Archie does not recognize his former friend: "This woman he had never known; she had somehow devoured his little friend, as the wolf ate up Red Riding-hood" (p. 500). Cather suggests here that society views such a woman in monstrous terms. When Doctor Archie, who originally encouraged her to go after what she wanted, complains that she doesn't have enough personal life, Thea explains:

> 'My dear doctor, I don't have any. Your work becomes your personal life. You are not much good until it does. It's like being woven into a big web. You can't pull away, because all your little tendrils are woven into the picture. It takes you up, and uses you, and spins you out; and that is your life. Not much else can happen to you. (p. 546)

The vision of the spider web is particularly apt here. Arachne, the mortal female who challenged the gods to match her weaving skills, was, after being acknowledged a superior artist, transformed into a monstrous spider. Thea has dared to challenge the gods.

When Doctor Archie leaves, she ponders her dread at meeting people from Moonstone: "A reality like Doctor Archie, poking up out of the past, reminded one of the disappointments and losses, of a freedom that was no more. . . ." (p. 514). This statement directly contradicts Cather's opening remarks that only on stage, in the very midst of her artistic endeavor, does she feel really free. On stage, Thea triumphs in the Wagnerian role of Sieglinde and her friendless life; she sings "of how the thing which was truly herself, 'bright as the day, rose to the surface' when in the hostile world she for the first time beheld her Friend [Siegmund]" (p. 58). In other words, she portrays the mythic role of the impassioned female on stage, a role she cannot live on earth, where she has had to reject the compassionate role of female, to accept the demon hate within her, and to strive ceaselessly for perfection.

If, as Cather asserts at the end of the novel, artistic growth is "a refining of the sense of truthfulness" (p. 571), a resistance to what Goethe called chaos, art is indeed expensive for all artists, but especially for the female who must be strong enough to be both demon and Faust, and yet continue to believe in her womanliness when she is obviously not the Eternal Woman.

Apologizing for the structure of this novel, Willa Cather writes, "The chief fault of the book is that it describes a descending curve; the life of a successful artist in the full tide of achievement is not so interesting as the life of a talented young girl . . ." (p. v). Rather than representing an artistic fault, what Cather calls the "descending curve" may represent a pattern particular to the woman's *Künstlerroman:* As the rating of her artistry rises on the social scale, the female artist may feel that the rating of her womanliness descends.

## PILGRIMAGE

That this feeling is unfounded or the result of a too-limiting categorization of womanhood is another concern of female writers. Dorothy Richardson, for instance, not only wrote a review entitled *"Das Ewig-Weibliche"* which warned writers against accepting and passing along Goethean concepts of "ladyhood," but also tried to offset the prevalent "masculine realism" by writing what she considered "feminine realism" in a thirteen-volume/chapter novel. In *Pilgrimage* (1915-1957) the heroine's intuitive perception of several sides of truth wars with her desire for finite knowledge and finite goals. That these two ways of knowing--intuitive and empirical--have been labeled "feminine" and "masculine" is unfortunate and disturbing to those who advocate fulfillment of human potential. Miriam, the heroine of *Pilgrimage*, strains against the limitation of such categorization but nevertheless suggests by her behavior and thoughts that she is abnormal for wanting to *do* rather than to *be*.

As a result of socialization, she identifies herself as "something between a man and a woman; looking both ways."[17] Women, according to Miriam, see "everything simultaneously. Unless they are the kind of woman who has been warped into seeing only one thing at a time. Scientifically. They are freaks. Women see in terms of life. Men in terms of things . . ." (III, 393). She believes that, in arguments, men establish their thesis, eliminate the unrelated elements, and reach their "truth" undisturbed by peripheral elements that may not jibe or by alternate views that challenge their thesis. She thinks that, in life, men set goals, eliminate unnecessary details (like relationships with people), and attain success.

21

Miriam, as a writer, has a two-directional vision which causes her to imagine herself freakish. When she performs aggressively or achieves a goal, she thinks of herself as manly. While practicing the piano, for instance, and playing well rather than prettily, she denies her femininity:

> *She had a clear conviction of manhood . . . that strange hard feeling that was always twining between her and the things people wanted her to do and to be. Manhood with something behind it that understood. This time it was welcome. It served. She asserted it, sadly feeling it mould the lines of her face.* (I, 471)

Despite her pleasure in accomplishment, she considers it manly and fears that her female face will be permanently disfigured. Her sadness stems from the cultural categorization of sexual roles.

Miriam later consciously rejects one image of women which has been reinforced by myth-builders like Goethe and by "all the literature in the world" (II, 219). In these books,

> *women stopped being people and went off into hideous processes. What for? What was it all for? Development. .......\* Sacred functions . . . highest possibilities . . . sacred for what? The hand that rocks the cradle rules the world? The Future of the Race? What world? What race? Men. . . . Nothing but men; for ever. . . . Books were poisoned. Art. All the achievements of men were poisoned at the root. ....... Life is poisoned, for women, at the very source.* (II, 220-22)

Miriam is ambivalent about society's view of women and about her own. Despite believing that women see in terms of life, she resents their image, in literature, as life processes. She would like to glorify their capacity for perception, not their biological processes. She is

---

\*All single-spaced ellipses will hereafter indicate my own omissions; Richardon's stream-of-consciousness passages will be quoted as printed.

rebelling against a concept of women *being* rather than *doing*. Because she will not conform to society's view of women, she has some doubts about her sexual identity.

If she pursues the path of physical experience *or* the one of intellectual exploration, she is denying her femininity. If she accepts a feminine role of nurturance, purity, softness, kindness, she denies half of her humanity, what she calls her "evil genius." As a result, Miriam describes herself as being in a deadlock: "A helpless going to and fro between two temperaments. A solid charwomanly commonplace kindliness, spread like a doormat at the disposal of everybody, and an intermittent perfect dilettantism that would disgust even the devil" (III, 245).

That these choices sound much like the Eternal Feminine and Faust's incessant striving is no accident. Miriam judges herself this harshly after viewing *Faust* with a male companion. Despite her hesitancy in accepting the feminine role ascribed to her, she recalls viewing the performance in an intuitive, receptive way, quite different from the reaction of her male companion. Whereas she is completely absorbed during the performance, delighting in the scenes, which she considers the visual "translation of the people, the actual picture of them as they were by themselves behind all the pother" (III, 200), Shatov criticizes the voice of the lead and delivers his personal interpretation of the philosophy, interrupting her appreciation and her intuitive understanding. The image she holds of herself as woman is nevertheless affected by the performance because later she moves "as into a brightness of light where she should stand visible to them both in a simplicity of golden womanhood, no longer herself, but his Marguerite, yet so differently fated, so differently identified with him . . ." (III, 201). She doesn't want to lose the strange radiance which surrounds and crowns her. By giving him a friendly goodnight, she learns the extent of her ability to charm: "She was overcome by the revelation of her power to bless without effort" (III, 203).

Most women confront this vision of themselves in a golden dream at some time. Miriam believes, "No one who has been inside it can ever be the same again or quite get out" (III, 202). Yet she is fully aware that his happiness, which stems from an adoration of her on the pedestal, is quite different from hers, which has to do with perceptivity. "To admit and acclaim her own would be the betrayal of a secret trust" (III, 202). Women must not demand their rights but can easily manipulate men if they play the feminine game. Miriam momentarily enjoys the power and the radiance that attend "The Eternal Woman," for Shatov, like Goethe, believes that "women can rise higher, and fall lower, than men" (III, 200). To destroy that belief would be treason, not only to her escort but to her own sense of womanhood; yet she cannot continue the game. She fears walking into his golden dream and vanishing in the blinding light of the temple he would construct around her, that ivory tower of light which would obliterate her artist-self. Later, she exclaims: "The prices of security, especially for women, are a damned sight too tall. Monstrous. Unthinkable. Who wouldn't sooner die than suffocate, even on an altar with incense perpetually rising?" (IV, 184).

Quelling the impulse to walk into Shatov's image of herself, to enter the golden vision of his dream and his admiration for her, she moves instead toward her inner, artistic being:

> *Something that was always there as if by appointment, waiting for one to get through to it away from everything in life. ........ It came out of oneself because it came only when one had been a long time alone. It was not oneself. It could not be God. It did not mind what you were or what you had done. It would be there if you had just murdered someone. It was only there when you had murdered everybody and everything and torn yourself away. Perhaps it was evil. One's own evil genius. But how could it make you feel so blissful?*
> *(II, 322)*

The dilemma of the female artist is vibrantly stated here. Miriam labels as morally sinful the reward which accompanies productive solitude. A woman is trained to believe that to shut off other people's needs or demands is to murder them. Although aloofness might be considered asocial for male or female, the degree of guilt which Miriam feels, a first-degree guilt of the murderess, indicates the identity crisis which women can experience when they act in their own self-interest. Such actions on behalf of the artistic self are, paradoxically, fatal to the self as woman.

There are socially-acceptable artistic roles women can play without feeling guilty. Despite her strong rejection of literature's idolatry of female biological processes, Miriam does some idolizing herself. She insists that most women are artists: " 'Whereas a few men here and there are creators, originators, *artists*, women are this all the time' " (III, 256). She claims that women have always been emancipated and that feminists, instead of complaining, should be admiring art forms of women:

> "The art of making atmospheres. It's as big an art as any other. Most women can exercise it, for reasons, by fits and starts. The best women work at it the whole of the time. Not one man in a million is aware of it. It's like air within the air. ....... Men live in it and from it all their lives without knowing." (III, 257)

According to Miriam, women have not been given proper credit or encouragement for their performance; instead of being told to find their true fulfillment in self-sacrifice, they should be told to find it in self-realization. She lauds *das ewig Weibliche,* not as a passive, nurturing capacity, but as an active, vital though indirect art form.

Judith Bardwick would explain that women produce art indirectly because they are unwilling to fight for independence. She claims, *"Normally, women will not participate in roles which threaten their affiliative needs, because these needs are critical in their basic concept of themselves."*[18] Consequently, rather than insist on the free time and privacy necessary to the creative artist, women direct their energy into hostessing or decorating. Carol Pearson also suggests that women have special cause to express their artistry indirectly in the fluid medium of life, acting out roles or creating atmospheres: "When the female artist acts indirectly, she not only avoids tragedy for herself and others but also integrates the passive heroine self with the self-expressive artist . . . ."[19] She fits Goethe's image of the Eternal Feminine.

Praising women who practice this traditional role of *das ewig Weibliche,* Miriam herself firmly refuses to exercise "the feminine art" (III, 258), which she claims is too exacting. Like other artists, she may also be rejecting "the feminine art" because society does not recognize it as aesthetically significant and because it is ephemeral. The artist of life cannot leave her work to future generations. Despite its fleeting quality, Miriam praises the demanding, grueling form of women's art.

She believes that women's actions have not received proper acclaim because men admire abstract reasoning and the development of things: "If making things is humanity's highest spiritual achievement, then women *are* secondary. . . . But *is* making pictures and bridges, and thumbscrews, humanity's highest spiritual achievement?" Miriam asks (IV, 464). Miriam's ambivalence is evident. She admires the mythic woman but prefers to capture life's moments in writing. She rejects Goethe's form of order and his concept of women in favor of her own.

Whereas Carol Pearson grants that a woman, acting indirectly as an artist of life, deserves praise for creating the illusion of order in a chaotic world, [20] Miriam vehemently denies that life is chaotic. Shortly after watching "hoar Chaos's fantastic son"[21] (Mephistopheles) in *Faust,* she argues that literature's way of stating is on a false foundation and that male authors have a faulty perception of life:

> *And if they want their old civilization to be anything but a dreary-weary puzzle, they must leave off imagining themselves a race of gods fighting against chaos, and thinking of women as part of the chaos they have to civilize. There isn't any "chaos." Never has been. It's the principal masculine illusion. (III, 219)*

Miriam is prompted to make this observation because she cannot admit that her heritage as a female is menial or less prestigious than the active male. Having the body of a female, she identifies physically with women. However, being intelligent, self-centered, independent, she does not identify positionally with them and therefore has to deny her womanhood. Consequently, she praises the actions of "The Eternal Woman" and simultaneously chides the patriarchy for enslaving women in this role of *das ewig Weibliche.*

Of course, Goethe is not solely responsible for this tradition; he is merely a link in a very strong chain. Nevertheless, such a tradition operates to constrain Miriam and to make her uneasy about her intellectual curiosity and her need for solitude, both considered unfeminine traits. She ironically reminds herself:

> *Disturbance about ideas would destroy the perfect serenity that was demanded of her. Be good, sweet maid, and let who will be clever. Easy enough if one were perpetually sustained by a strong and adoring hand. Perhaps more difficult really to be good than to be clever. (II, 390)*

Miriam's cleverness is much more natural than is the suppression of her intellectual spirit.

Trying to convince herself that intellectual curiosity makes her neither unwomanly nor evil, she muses:

> *Adam had not faced the devil. He was stupid first, and afterwards a coward and a cad . . . 'the divine curiosity of Eve. . . .' Some parson had said that. . . . Perhaps man would turn around one day and see, what they were like. Eve had not been unkind to the devil; only Adam and God. (I, 459)*

If women are naturally receptive, kind, passive, they must then accept completely. Evil, good, all of life is included; no exclusions are possible. In such a state, art--defined by patriarchal tradition as honed, shaped, and directed--would not exist. Neither would chaos. Feminine realism would include it all. Polarities and dichotomies would be presented in such a moving form as to create wholes, much the way positive and negative energy moves in an atom and creates a whole.

The structure of this novel reflects Richardson's insistence on such feminine realism. Rather than a novel of episodes during which Miriam develops a sensitive awareness or an understanding of the world which can then lift her to an ivory tower, the heroine's conflict continues even at the end. Drawn by various beacons, she bounces from barrier to barrier and from soaring vision to vision. Her consistency is this perpetual motion, a wavering journey caused by her inability to resolve internal tensions of an abstract nature as they surface when she assumes particular cultural roles.

27

Ruling out the possibilities of role-playing as pianist, certified teacher, governess, painter, dental secretary, Lycurgan, Jew's wife, doctor's wife, feminist, hostess, international socialite, free-lover, ex-seminarian's wife, Quaker, and Quaker's wife, Miriam eventually settles into her role as a writer. She must then express the revolving polarity of such abstract concepts as masculine and feminine, solitude and companionship, Toryism and socialism, language and silence, subjectivity and objectivity, marriage and freedom, ecstacy and peace, free will and determinism, as well as the metaphoric entities of walled gardens and open spaces, or light and darkness. Rather than resolve these polarities, Richardson *revolves* them, keeping them in suspension to emphasize life's fullness rather than its directness.

Criticizing the method and describing the difficulty of establishing rapport "with two thousand pages containing the flotsam and jetsam of consciousness, fragments of experience, emotions conveyed in emotion-limiting words," Leon Edel seals the fate of *Pilgrimage* by saying that successful reading of it depends considerably on the reader's sex. [22] His criticism reflects *Faust's* last lines, "Human discernment / Here is passed by." Edel suggests that the reader needs to be a superhuman or a subhuman woman in order to comprehend this "feminine realism." Ordinary human discernment cannot pierce the veil. Both Richardson and Goethe praise womanhood, but Goethe praises its *being* whereas Richardson praises its *doing*. As Edel suggests, her work does not follow the traditional mythic pattern. But, as Miriam explains, "If women had been the recorders of things from the beginning it would all have been the other way round . . ." (II, 251).

## ORLANDO

In a mode entirely different from Richardon's realism, Virginia Woolf metaphorically suggested the problems of a female artist by creating *Orlando* (1928), a *Künstlerroman* and a fantasy. Freed from conventions of realism or of mythic traditions, Virginia Woolf can create a hero-ine, by having the main character change sex from male to female in midstream. The narrator suggests that such a transformation is more realistic than it seems: "Different though the sexes are, they intermix. In every human being a vacillation from one sex to the other takes place . . . ." [23] Although this particular passage reinforces

Woolf's insistence that a person write without consideration of her sex, the protagonist's experiences depend a great deal on society's perception of her sex. She must change attire to play different roles. Wearing men's clothes, she can be active and accumulate experiences directly. When she wears petticoats, she partakes of life's pleasures passively and indirectly.

Just as Miriam falls under the spell of hostessing and emphasizes its artistry, Woolf also places her heroine in this arena and describes its enchantment:

> The hostess is our modern Sibyl. She is a witch who lays her guests under a spell. In this house they think themselves happy; in that witty; in a third profound. It is all an illusion (which is nothing against it, for illusions are the most valuable and necessary of all things, and she who can create one is among the world's greatest benefactors) . . . . (p. 199)

Goethe would agree that such illusions are attractive. Faust admires Margarete's domicile--neat, orderly, peaceful--an abode of the Eternal Feminine. The female artist is enticed by the atmosphere and by the suggestion that her womanliness is somehow dependent on her ability to create such atmospheres. But the hostess creates only a mirage, and the female artist usually strives for a more permanent monument to her talent. The socially-accepted form of female artistry does not suit Orlando.

Although her sexual change and span of life break conventional boundaries, she too suffers restraints as a woman. Her activities are circumscribed. Woolf ironically explains: "When we are writing the life of a woman, we may, it is agreed, waive our demand for action and substitute love instead" (p. 268). The capacity to love is the prime trait of the Eternal Woman. Margarete's steadfast love carries Faust's soul beyond the human realm. This tradition of the passive, patient, and loving woman constrains female writers. At some time in their lives, they usually react in print or in person to Byron's statement that love is a woman's whole existence. Virginia Woolf is no exception. Her narrator suggests that to be well-received by the readers, even an intellectual female character like Orlando must be described as thinking of a man, for "as long as she thinks of a man, nobody objects to a woman thinking" (p. 268).

Despite the inclusion of such remarks concerning the realistic portrayal of a woman who is also an artist, the work remains an obvious fantasy, a portrait of the ultimate writer, who has "the strength of a man and a woman's grace" (p. 138). One very important element of this fantasy is that the hero-ine can both *do* and *be*: the pant-legged Orlando enjoys experiences and the crinolined Orlando, passive and modest, can remain in the ivory tower. Both create a work of art. Without such sexual transformation and a life-span of centuries, the feat would be difficult. To fantasize is to wish temporarily for a different life. As Patricia Spacks comments, "Fantasy is the best protection against the imperfections of reality." [24] By choosing to escape reality in this literary form, Woolf indicates the tensions a female writer normally faces and sidesteps a direct confrontation with them.

In addition, Woolf suggests the conflict of the woman writer in two images at the end of the book. Orlando becomes fragmented, floating from present to past, from observation to memory, from external to internal observation. This fragmentation may happen to anyone, particularly to an artist, but especially to a female writer. As the narrator explains, "Everybody can multiply from his own experience the difficult terms which his different selves have made with him" (pp. 308-09). But Orlando, moving distractedly through the empty house, stops by the tapestry which is "the frail indomitable heart of the immense building" (p. 318). This needlework (once a woman's art form) depicts Daphne being chased by the hunter and escaping by transformation into a laurel tree. Unlike Margarete, Daphne runs from, not toward, her ravishment. Her escape into the symbol of poetry is purchased at the price of her womanhood, indeed, of her life. The tapestry's being at the center of the large structure indicates the importance of the tension which influences the writer. It is the central motivating force of the work.

The final scene of *Orlando* takes place in a world where men fly. Orlando's lover descends from a plane, but over his head, the wild goose flies. The ecstasy Orlando feels upon seeing Shel mingles with the sweet anguish of being haunted by the goose: " 'Always it flies out to sea and always I fling after it words like nets . . . . And sometimes there's an inch of silver--six words--in the bottom of the net. But never the great fish who lives in the coral groves' " (p. 313). Woolf's depiction of the descending Shelmerdine and the flying goose is a definite reversal of Goethe's image--the Eternal Female lifting Faust to salvation with a burst of attendant poetry. Men and the spirit of poetry fly, perhaps through the graces of the Eternal Woman. Virgina Woolf suggests that female writers remain below. Commenting on the structure in *Orlando,* the narrator explains, "The truth is that when we write of a woman, everything is out of place--culminations and perorations; the accent never falls where it does with a man" (p. 312).


## SAVE ME THE WALTZ

The pattern of descent and subsequent inability to surface victoriously also occurs in Zelda Fitzgerald's *Save Me the Waltz* (1932), a novel which specifically refers to the Faust legend. The artistic urges of the heroine, Alabama Beggs, are dramatically contrasted with those of the hero, David Knight. Carving their names in a doorpost, he marks: "David, . . . David, David, Knight, Knight, Knight, and Miss Alabama Nobody." [25] The egotistical carving, accomplished with the sexually-implicit knife, reflects a patriarchal world in which a female relinquishes her identity for the rewards of male protection and the questionable power of being able to inflate the male ego.

David informs Alabama that he will bring her to the fairy mill of New York City: "You are my princess and I'd like to keep you shut forever in an ivory tower for my private delectation" (p. 40). After the third time he writes this statement, Alabama objects and asks him not to mention the imprisoning tower again; later, as his wife, she wants to be treated as a princess and put in David's pocket. Then he complains that the pocket probably has a hole in it because she's forgotten to mend it. Alabama, like Miriam, wants the attention and the adoration but not the imprisonment of the ivory tower.

As a male artist, David is free to vie for the approval or attention of society. Alabama is restricted by social conventions. In a whirlwind of society with too few praiseworthy goals, too much emphasis on being attractive, carefree, and decorative, she loses the respect of her parents. As the wife of David and the mother of Bonnie, she still has nothing to do, for even her child is charged to a nanny so that Alabama can ride the social merry-go-round with David. The contrast between Alabama's ceaseless activity and Faust's is crystallized by Zelda Fitzgerald in one sentence: "The village band played 'Faust' and merry-go-round waltzes in a round pavillion by the sea" (p. 89). This juxtaposition is not coincidental, for the author later forces Alabama to choose between personal relationships and art; she must turn her back on the former if she is to dance in the *Faust* ballet.

All artists must deal with the dilemma of solitude vs. companionship. David, too, needs to be alone to work in peace; but his need is expected. On the other hand, he expects Alabama to cooperate and make life comfortable for him. Alabama must fight against tradition and her natural desire for love, which is dependent upon that tradition. As she says: " 'It's very difficult to be two simple people at once, one who wants to have a law to itself and the other who wants to keep all the nice old things and be loved and safe and protected' " (p. 56).

Unable to soar in this conventional world which views women as flowers, things which *are* rather than *do,* she asks David to love her anyway, explaining, " 'I did so want to be paid, somehow, for my soul' " (p. 68). The implication is that Faust actually makes the bargain and establishes the conditions under which he will lose his soul; Alabama loses it by marrying and by becoming a part of the social whirlwind around her.

Eventually turning her back on this merry-go-round of life, she works furiously as a ballet dancer, a role which is permissible to the slight but dedicated female. She achieves minor acclaim in the *Faust* ballet, fully aware that her success is relative to her looks--the other dancers are heavy, old, and ugly. Even so, the dedication to this art causes her to be drained physically and emotionally. Her relationship with her daughter suffers, for Bonnie prefers to be with David, comfortably taking advantage of his success, rather " 'than with Mummy's success in Italy' " (p. 189). The child does not even feel her mother's presence, only her "success." But the comfort that Bonnie feels is dependent upon her allowing others to rule her existence, upon her giving up her soul, in fact.

Going home from a ballet performance, Bonnie rides in David's limousine: "They drove through the black impenetrable shadows clouding the road like fumes from an alchemist's laboratory and sped across the gleam of the open mountain top" (p. 187). Since Alabama advises Bonnie "not to be a back-seat driver about life" (p. 190) and Zelda describes David's car as a "death-car" driven in a Faustian setting, the implication seems clear. Both Bonnie and Alabama sell their souls to the devil if they settle for the traditional role of woman, dependent upon the artistry of her man.

After a case of blood poisoning aborts her chances of reaching an artistic goal, Alabama sorrowfully returns to domesticity. Kept in an ivory tower or playing the role of a fount, a giver of life, women can pretend they are goddesses. A woman's struggling ceaselessly and independently to achieve the ivory tower is less glorified than Faustian striving and less rewarding if there is no gentle, pure soul to intercede.

The final phrases of the novel underscore the ugliness and pitifulness of a woman's climb toward artistic heights. Emptying ash trays, Alabama likens their emptiness to her own. Whereas the male artist might be envisioned rising like a phoenix from these ashes, Alabama describes herself in passive terms. She has made her only attempt to fly from the conventional role she now accepts.

Such a final scene, depicting the domesticity rather than the flight of the female artist, occurs in several novels. After many "Faustian" struggles--some exciting, some dull, some sordid, and some imaginary --the female artist is frequently stopped by domestic ties from continuing her journey toward freedom or toward artistic expression.


## THE ODYSSEY OF KATINOU KALOKOVICH

For instance, Natalie Petesch, in *The Odyssey of Katinou Kalokovich* (1974), depicts the struggle of a woman who wants to devote her life to art and to avoid entrapment in an orderly domicile like Margarete's. In this novel, the adolescent heroine reacts negatively to the image of herself as a pure "Eternal Woman," the tenant of an ivory tower. In her initial sexual encounter, she is aroused and then quickly abandoned by the male who discovers she is a virgin. The narrator explains the significance of this act in Faustian terms:

> *The experience had left her with the conviction that virginity was a handicap which falsely differentiated her from men: by limiting her experience it limited her humanity; it therefore must ultimately limit her as an artist: she wished to be a part of all that she had met,\* not an innocent girl in a pretty frock, ignorant of life.* [26]

Deliberately fleeing from imprisonment in this ivory tower, she survives an early marriage of economic necessity which makes her feel like a prostitute, a pregnancy which occurs despite medically prescribed birth-control precautions, an illegal abortion which almost kills her, and subsequent sexual violations by her estranged husband while she is still recuperating from the abortion. Although these activities seem a dynamic part of life, note that her role in each case is passive. She has to struggle to escape both the ivory tower and the sacred fount, for she is used in each. Her evasion proves futile, however, for she must eventually return home to tend a baby sister when her mother is confined to an asylum.

At home, she finds that her art is adversely affected by tradition and by her immediate experience. While painting, she stops abruptly, realizing what has happened: "She had fallen face-first into a puddle of Sentimentality. She was painting the so-called simple joys of Home, Family, and Property. She had been tempted into the ultimate trap, the Tenderness Trap" (p. 215). Petesch suggests that the mythic image of motherhood and society's image of women as tendering or mothering creatures combine to limit or to circumscribe the artistic output of women. Her heroine is continually rebelling against that tradition and being drawn unwillingly into it.


## THE PUBLIC IMAGE

Whereas Faust is redeemed by the intercession of several "mothers," including Gretchen and the Virgin Mary, the mythic image of mother-

---

\*This reference is to Tennyson's *Ulysses,* who, like Faust, was also a doer--a seeker of knowledge and experience.

hood operates to damn the female artist externally and internally. In *The Public Image*, Muriel Spark depicts a modern day Galatea (the statue rather than the sea nymph), a movie actress who, like Helen, is the idol of her continent. Her personal Pygmalion claims, " 'It's what I began to make of you that you've partly become.' " [27] The relationship between private life, public image, and personality becomes murky when Annabel Christopher, the heroine, bears a child in an attempt to solidify her image as a successful actress and woman, playing the roles of wife and mother. When, out of emotional and professional jealousy, her husband rebels in his role, she becomes frightened "at the whole mythology that had vapoured so thickly about her . . ." (p. 46). Eventually abandoned by her envious husband, Annabel redefines *betrayal* as setting up a myth, reacting against it, and then exploding the myth, thereby destroying a human being in the process.

As artist and mother, she is abused, blackmailed, and dethroned. Fleeing from the mythic and public image, she is depicted at the airport statically poised between the Sacred Fount and the Ivory Tower, a foot in the base of each:

> *Waiting for the order to board, she felt both free and unfree. The heavy weight of the bags was gone; she felt as if she was still, curiously, pregnant with the baby, but not pregnant in fact. She was pale as a shell . . . . Nobody recognized her as she stood, having moved the baby to rest on her hip, conscious also of the baby in a sense weightlessly and perpetually within her, as an empty shell contains, by its very structure, the echo and harking image of former and former seas. (p. 192)*

Weighted by the cultural and biological condition of each role, she can eliminate only one. She waits passively for a flight that will remove her from circumstances which she may never escape. The mother remains grounded.

## THE GOLDEN NOTEBOOK

Looming as a mythic model for women, Goethe's *ewig Weibliche* is difficult to abandon. The creature is seductive. Anna Wulf, in *The*

*Golden Notebook,* recognizes Saul Green's yearning for the mythic woman and her own propensity toward fulfilling that role rather than establishing a new one. She explains,

> *He was looking for this wise, kind, all-mother figure*
> *who is also sexual playmate and sister; and because I*
> *had become part of him, this is what I was looking for*
> *too, both for myself, because I need her, and because*
> *I wanted to become her.* [28]

Relating to Saul as a woman, she feels compelled to fulfill his dreams. Despite the fact that she can dispel the mythic woman intellectually, she cannot abandon her emotionally. She mourns, "I knew this with my intelligence, and yet I sat there in my dark room, . . . longing with my whole being for that mythical woman, longing to be her, but for Saul's sake" (p. 502).

If women walk into the golden dream and become the pure, the mythic, the healing, the Eternal Woman, they run the risk of being denounced for the very role they adopt. Many males react violently, as does Saul, against "Women the jailors, the consciences, the voice of society . . ." (p. 539). In such a situation, the role available then becomes a negative one, "the woman betrayed" (p. 539). But the word "betrayed" has a new meaning. Goethe's *Faust* involves the demonic principle that uses females and then abandons them. But Doris Lessing and Muriel Spark, twentieth-century female writers, depict another kind of betrayal--that which occurs when women accept myths established by writers like Goethe. Both betrayals involve woman's necessity for love, but the principle differs.

Anna, in musing about the happiness she has felt in love-making, asks: "What is this thing we need so much? (By we, meaning women.) And what is it worth?" (p. 508). When her paramour leaves her, she feels betrayed because she knows he has already forgotten the happiness of their moment together. Lessing, the artist, is obviously speaking through her heroine when she writes:

> *But I saw this not merely as denying Anna, but as*
> *denying life itself. I thought that somewhere here is a*
> *fearful trap for women, but I don't yet understand*

*what it is. For there is no doubt of the new note women
strike, the note of being betrayed. It's in the books they
write, in how they speak, everywhere, all the time. It is
a solemn, self-pitying organ note. It is in me, Anna
betrayed, Anna unloved, Anna whose happiness is
denied, and who says, not: Why do you deny me,
but why do you deny life? (p. 509)*

If females adopt the mythical role of loving, life-giving "femininity,"
they will perceive rejection of themselves as rejection of that principle.
Accepting the myth will allow them no individuality, only a feeling of
being trapped in life processes.

Because women frequently define themselves by way of their relationships to men, female writers must especially guard against creating
"the woman altogether better" than themselves (p. 545) and thereby
perpetuating myths of *das ewig Weibliche*. As Anna explains:

*I was thinking that quite possibly these marvellous,
generous things we walk side by side with in our
imaginations could come in existence, simply because
we need them, because we imagine them. Then I began
to laugh because of the distance between what I was
imagining and what in fact I was . . . . (p. 545)*

This distance mockingly calls the artist to span it in some way. To do so,
she must ignore other pleas, enlist Mephistopheles' aid, entertain
chaos, or generally destroy something. This necessity places the
woman between two familiar horns. Referring to Rank's dictum that
women are not destroyers and therefore not artists, Ellen Peck Killoh
identifies the dilemma:

*Woman and artist are two mutually exclusive categories
because women are by definition preservers while
artists must be able to destroy. . . . Such received
authorities, foist ready-made conflicts onto any woman
who would dare to be a writer. One would like to throw
out the whole dichotomy, but in practice this has not
been so easy.* [29]

37

Dorothy Richardson tried to evade the dichotomy by denying the existence of chaos; ironically, her work is labeled chaotic. To create a work of art is to choose. To choose is to deny other possibilities. To be "eternally feminine" is to recognize or accept all. The tension between these two poles is dramatized by Anna Wulf's madness in *The Golden Notebook*.

She cannot bear to hurt the feelings of others, to evict the homosexual boarders who are taking advantage of her good nature, or to deny men who "need" her. To "a person who continually destroys the possibilities of a future because of the numbers of alternative viewpoints" (p. 555), art becomes impossible. Anna reads this information in the newspaper. She becomes impotent as a writer when she comprehends the relative value of words. Attempting to write down her illumination, she cannot decide the category, the proper notebook, in which to record it.

Having perceived with "womanly intuition" that the papers she has been pasting on the wall are fragments of print offering unassimilable information, she also reacts "womanly" in her inability to strip the walls or to destroy the wordy accretion of wallpaper. She relies upon Milt, the American, to service her in three ways--to strip the walls, to make her feel temporarily protected and cared for, and to serve her sexually. His role is active, hers passive. Yet, paradoxically, he asks her to remain perceptive as though she were all-powerful, the Woman Eternal: "Anna, I need it. When someone needs something you give it to them" (p. 561). When she eventually rises from her passive stupor, Milt insists that she and women in general must continue to "take on" men because women are tougher and kinder. The myth must not be destroyed. Even if women *have* grown tougher and kinder, they are trapped then by that fact.

Still tortured by the need to speak in a world where speech is incomprehensible, Anna turns away from her writing to contribute actively to social reform. The golden notebook, begun by Anna, is finished by Saul, the male writer. Her conception of herself as woman makes her view relationships to others as far more important than such Faustian striving. For female artists, the dilemma remains.

# SUMMARY

While upholding her womanly role, the female writer must somehow balance her bodily needs, her intellectual longing, her creative and her procreative urges, her protective and her demonic impulses. Her art may emerge as lacking traditional form and therefore "featureless," as the gift of chaos, as a controlled but descending pattern, as a golden notebook created from the knowledge that truth spills over and cannot be contained in pigeonholes of blue, black, yellow, and red, or as a fantasy of spanned centuries and sexual transformations.

If there is an ur-principle of *mythos,* it is continually being rewritten and reformed. The Miltonic view of woman, a weak vessel through whom the devil tempted man, is replaced in *Faust* by Goethe's view of Woman Eternal. This mythic woman is kind enough to forgive the man his betrayal of her and good enough to renew his spirit, which has been "soiled" while striving for superior knowledge. Goethe glorified but polarized male and female spirits. Women writers of the twentieth century may rework the *Faust* myth to focus on the meaninglessness of incessant striving, on the untruthfulness of Faust's goal-directed ambition, on the productive restlessness of an androgynous spirit, or on the rebellion of a female Dr. Faustina who wants but does not need the nurture of an understanding male. In the process, the authors who continually renew this myth are also redefining the universal pattern in literature and in life.

## Chapter III

# DEMETER/PERSEPHONE AND THE ARTIST AS HEROINE

> *"How can the creative impulse be nurtured in women--*
> *we, who have forgotten our myths, who have no*
> *rituals from which to proceed?*
> *Who will our goddesses and heroines be?"* [1]
> *--Phyllis Chesler*

> *"Women are trained to be rape victims."*
> *"A good heroine is a dead heroine . . . ."* [2]
> *--Susan Brownmiller*

## BACKGROUND

Whereas the male artist can identify with traditional heroes like Faust without jeopardizing his self-image or his sexual identity, the female writer is hampered by the heritage of patriarchal myths in a society which arbitrarily excludes her from various experiences, sets her on a pedestal or in a pigsty, and otherwise causes ambivalence about her self-image whether she follows its traditions or rejects the "heroinizing" of its myths. Within the last decade, female psychologists, sociologists, philosophers, and literary critics have tried to relocate or to identify traditions they can label their own. In *The Female Imagination,* Patricia Spacks reported that she perceived feelings of anger and inadequacy in the content and style of women's literature. Anaïs Nin believed that insecurity was a problem for most women writers; in many of her essays and journals, she exhorted them and herself to write from the inner core of feminine being. In *Man's World, Woman's Place,* Elizabeth Janeway suggested that role conflict might constitute that "core" and give unity to women's traditional roles and therefore to women's literature. In *Against Our Will,* Susan Brownmiller saw that fear of rape directed women's lives. In *Literary Women,* Ellen Moers traced "the deep creative strategies of the literary mind at work upon the fact of female"[3] and unearthed some particularly feminine ways of handling imagery.

A half-century ago, Virginia Woolf claimed that while writers appealing to the largest audience draw from a bisexual or androgynous imagination, women's lives have specific patterns and values which will inform their work.[4] This pattern should be most evident in autobiographical novels of the artist, particularly in the *Künstlerromanen* written by and about women.

As I read these novels, I find one common experience that informs them. All women are daughters. Some are mothers. The mother/daughter relationship is often central to the novel of the artist as heroine. To understand why this relationship is so important, one must know something of its complexities.

Psychologists, psychiatrists, and theorists of psychology agree that the mother/child relationship is crucial to either sex. Psychologists claim that, in infancy, children experience themselves first as one with their mother and later must cope with the process of individuation and with the object-loss that occurs when nourishment or her presence is withheld. Nancy Chodorow explains subsequent development:

> *Thus, as children of either sex attempt to gain independence, . . . they must do this by consciously or unconsciously rejecting their mother (and people like her) and the things she is associated with. This fact, and the cultural institutions and emphases that it seems to entail, has different consequences for boys and for girls.*[5]

The consequences are complex. A major part of the growing-up process involves gender identification or the internalization of a sex-role. Because children, when young, are usually continually in the presence

41

of women, gender identification is relatively easy for a young girl. But a child's relationship to parents is both positional and personal. Studies gathered by Chodorow reveal consequential difficulties for women in the processes of separation and individuation:

In a patriarchal society, a boy gains status in the outside world by giving up the mother and identifying with the father. For a girl, becoming a woman means assuming the sex of her mother, to whom society offers few rewards and whose own self-esteem is consequently often low. Even if the daughter likes the mother personally, she may dislike her mother's role and rebel against assuming a similar position.

Moreover, a woman's biosexual experiences stall the processes of separation and individuation. A woman finds it difficult to develop a separate ego, a "me" distinct from "not me," in relation, for instance, to her blood, to milk from her breasts, to a child once part of her body (and hence to all children), perhaps even to a man, a part of whom she's held within her body. By example, a mother encourages not individuation but interdependence. In becoming a woman, a young girl assumes a body similar to her mother's, a body which has nurtured.

Formerly free and relatively independent as a "tomboy," a girl entering puberty may react ambivalently toward these bodily functions and toward the role to which they tie her. Needing love from her mother, she may also feel the opposing need to set boundaries between the two of them. One way is to project her own negative feelings on her parent. [7]

The mother may use this technique, in reverse. Even if she doesn't, she may pass along negative attitudes toward her body. According to Phyllis Chesler, many females are trained to "mother" yet "are conditioned not to like women and/or the female body." She claims that biological mothers are often "phobic about lesbianism," "jealous of their daughters' youth" or freedom, nervous or angry about their secondary status in a patriarchal system, and necessarily "harsh in training their daughters to be 'feminine' in order . . . to survive." [8]
Indeed, studies have revised the old notion that parents are usually warm and tender toward girls and harsh to boys; recent data indicate cross-sexed responses which become more pronounced as the girl's sex characteristics become more obvious in adolescence. [9]  This is not to

suggest that such harshness or withdrawal by the mother is completely detrimental to the daughter. Other studies reveal that "the most independent, aggressive and competitively achievement-motivated girls are those who receive the least affection from their mothers."[10] Judith Bardwick notes, "A little alienation [real or imagined] seems to have big repercussions."[11] But these women are often prompted to achieve by a need to increase self-esteem or to obtain love. Ironically, success may, in turn, cause such a woman to doubt her "femininity." Thus, women seem to restrict themselves in an attempt to meet their affiliative needs. As a result, Phyllis Chesler claims, "Most women are glassed into infancy . . . by an unmet need for maternal nurturance."[12] Shulamith Firestone concurs, adding that, whether the girl intuits or actually experiences it, "the mother's rejection, occurring for different reasons, produces an insecurity about her identity in general, creating a lifelong need for approval."[13]

If one holds in mind the complexities involved in a woman's psychic development--the difficulty of establishing biosexual boundaries, the problems of individuation, the seemingly negative consequences of gender identification--one can understand her contradictory longings: the wish to be "mothered" and the countervailing need to establish her own identity, unhampered by a self-image which depends on identification with her mother or the motherly role.

A woman's relationships with men do not sever those she has with her mother nor do they sharpen the focus of her mirror-image. They may even confuse her further. Either from her mother or on her own, she learns her potential power--awesome not only to others but to herself as well. She experiences physical changes--menses, pregnancy, childbirth, lactation, and menopause--all of which magically transform her relationships with others, but also affect her, without control. She learns seductive powers that can transform a man physically but can unleash a male force destructive to her body and spirit. On the other hand, she learns or senses that her own seductive power must not overwhelm her lover lest she appear as vagina dentata and deflate or terrify him. As a result of her relationships with men, which depend to a great extent on those with her mother, she eventually incorporates a self-image which Dorothy Dinnerstein describes as follows:

*The woman feels herself on the one hand a supernatural*
*being, before whom the man bluffs, quails, struts, and*
*turns stony for fear of melting; and she feels herself on*
*the other hand a timid child, unable to locate in herself*
*the full magic power which as a baby she felt in her*
*mother. The man can seem to her to fit her childhood*
*ideal of a male adult [at least temporarily] far better*
*than she herself fits her childhood ideal of a female*
*adult.* [14]

In her ambivalence, identifying while not necessarily wanting to identify with her mother, a woman relates to her lover as both mother (superior and powerful) and child (inferior and powerless).

Because women are trained not to be themselves (especially around men), but to be "like mothers,"[15] individuation is difficult if not impossible. During biological motherhood, a woman is vicariously once again both child and mother, returning to a primordial state, experiencing unity and object-loss relationships, and repeating a cycle which transcends the limitations of time. Suggesting that she trancends even the beginnings of time, Erich Neumann claims, "The woman experiences herself first and foremost as the source of life."[16] Although such claims glorify womanhood, they also mold women to nurture or "mother" (even if they reject the biological condition of motherhood), deter females in general from an interest in the self, and may hamper the female artist in particular from developing a necessary narcissism. As Carol Pearson explains, "Unlike the male artist . . . the female artist faces internal conflicts between the selfless role of the heroine and the self-expressive role of the artist."[17]

## DEMETER/PERSEPHONE MYTH

Whereas the establishment of identity is difficult and central for any woman, it is of the utmost importance for women writing autobiographical novels of the artist as heroine. When one examines these novels as a genre, the relationship of mother and daughter looms in mythic proportions. Along with the poet Adrienne Rich, the psychologist Phyllis Chesler, and the literary critic Joseph Blotner, I have discovered that an appreciation of the Demeter/Persephone myth provides insights to women's lives and their art. Although none of the novelists discussed in the following sections have specifically used the Demeter/Persephone myth, it synthesizes the mother/daughter cathexis and the mysteries related to that relationship. I label the main figures in the myth Demeter/Persephone because the two blur, just as the boundaries between mother and child fade in each woman. The name *Demeter* identifies the "mother" and *Persephone* means "Kore" or "maiden."

I shall briefly summarize the myth because, like many other elements of female culture, the role these figures played in the rituals of Eleusis are forgotten or buried. Edith Hamilton, in *Mythology*, explains: "The chief part of the ceremony which took place in the precincts of the temple has never been described. Those who beheld it were bound by a vow of silence and they kept it so well that we know only stray bits of what was done."[18] The Homeric Hymns and other extant versions provide essential information about the myth, but reports differ and the details remain unclear. Supposedly, Demeter was the goddess empowered to bring forth grain. She withheld her gifts from the earth when she lost her only daughter, Persephone. She eventually learned from the sun or from birds that, enticed by the Narcissus or while lilies, the maiden strayed from companions; Pluto (King of Hades) spied, ravished, and abducted her. Mourning, Demeter rested at Eleusis near a well. Annoyed by the mortal behavior of the local people, she nevertheless had compassion, revealed herself as a goddess, and commanded them to build a temple for her at Eleusis. After its completion, she sat there, longing for her daughter, wasting away, and at the same time depriving the earth of its grain. After several pleas to Demeter, Zeus realized that his brother Pluto must release the girl; he ordered that she be returned to Demeter provided Persephone had eaten nothing during her stay in the underworld. Because she partook of a few pomegranate seeds--some versions say at the coaxing of Pluto-- she was doomed to return seasonally to Hades. Only one-half to two-thirds of the year could she spend with her mother. Edith Hamilton claims that Demeter was a good and kind goddess, happy to have Persephone returned to her, and sorry for the desolation she had caused. Acknowledging her relationship to men, she made the fields rich, chose Triptolemus, a prince of Eleusis, as her ambassador, and instructed men to sow corn.

I agree with Hamilton that sorrow is the foremost emotion in this myth, despite the conciliatory ending. Demeter, goddess of harvest, saw her daughter die each year. Persephone, the radiant maiden, knew how brief that beauty was, became aware of male power and cleverness (prompting her to "eat the seed"), and, separated from her mother, lost both her freedom and her gaiety. Previously aware of her mother's power, she learned of her mother's helplessness and sorrow. The core of the mysteries supposedly involved Demeter's quality as her daughter's mother;[19] but, in searching for her girl-child, the goddess searched for a part of herself as well. The Eleusinian mysteries may have appealed not only as an intellectual acknowledgment of the split which precedes finding again, of the "disjoined continuation"[20] that every daughter experiences in relation to her mother, but also as a celebration and acknowledgment of the fact that every woman contains within herself both mother and daughter. Jung believed that the celebration was entirely female; whereas other myths might be male fantasies or anima projections, these rituals, he thought, were alien to man. "In fact," he wrote, "the psychology of the Demeter cult has all the features of a matriarchal order of society, where the man is an indispensable but on the whole disturbing factor."[21] Kerényi, among others, disagreed with Jung, for he believed that men took part in these ceremonies and that the happy marriage of the ravished maiden was the prototype of all marriages.[22] Whether the myth is patriarchal or matriarchal, it afforded a cathartic and rejuvenating effect for the feminine psyches of Greek culture. Though modern women might deny the same effect now, the myth still positively influences some women. Adrienne Rich, for one, writes: "The images of the prepatriarchal goddess-cults did one thing: they told women that power, awesomeness, and centrality were theirs by nature, not by privilege or miracle; the female was primary."[23] Whatever its effect on women in ancient times, the myth crystallizes several tensions existing in mother-daughter relationships today.

Demeter is both the Terrible and the Good Mother, a split we all recognize in our own mothers. The personification of fecundity, nurturance, and loving concern, she also is powerfully awesome, persevering in her desire to maintain control over her offspring, vengeful, and able to withhold sustenance. Though not completely successful, Demeter challenges the patriarchal order on behalf of her daughter.

Innocent, beautiful, and radiant, Persephone is, by name and action, the eternal maiden. Yet she is also sorrowful, split between male and female lovers, between mother and husband, in their battle for control. She epitomizes the childlike need for nurturance that so many women experience. As Adrienne Rich explains:

> There was, is, in most of us, a girl-child still longing for a woman's nurture, tenderness, and approval, a woman's power exerted in our defence, a woman's smell and touch and voice, a woman's strong arms around us in moments of fear and pain. [24]

Yet most of us also suffer what she terms "matrophobia," a fear of becoming one's mother. We wish to be free of our mothers' bondage, to become individuals. Adrienne Rich's perceptive view of this struggle within herself and other strong women leads her to make two generalizations. About women in general, she claims, "The loss of the daughter to the mother, the mother to the daughter, is the essential female tragedy." [25] Speaking as an artist, she offers insights to the mother-daughter-artist relationship: "The woman . . . artist born of a family-centered mother may . . . feel that her mother cannot understand or sympathize with the imperatives of her life; or that her mother has preferred and valued a more conventional daughter, or a son." [26] To that I would add, the woman artist born of a mother with suppressed or frustrated creative urges also struggles in the mother-daughter mold. Good or bad, the relationship energizes many women's novels and forms the core of most of their *Künstlerromanen*. In these autobiographical novels focusing on the difficulties or growth of the artist, the heroines must always wrestle with mothers, with daughters, or with their own identity in either role. The myth provides a clear view of the nature of those roles.

In addition to the primordial relationship, the myth also deals with perhaps the most violent (if not the most common) interaction between men and women--the act of rape. Philip Wheelwright, commenting on the various rites of passage, notes that rape is at the core of the Eleusinian mysteries. In trying to explain why, he writes:

> Evidently because rape symbolizes one of the most important and emotionally arresting 'passages' in

47

*human experience--the passage from the pure state of*
*virginity through the shock of violation and attaining*
*to the happy issue of periodic motherhood. Demeter's*
*descent into Hades connects symbolically the rape*
*archetype with the even more universal archetype of*
*death and life in alternation.* 27

Wheelwright's masculine bias allows him to ignore the horrendous psychological effect of rape on the victim and on society, to overlook the fact that virgins are not the only victims of rape, to identify rape as an act perpetrated only on women, to equate death and rape (perhaps a fate worse than . . .), and to connect a *happy* issue of "periodic motherhood" with such violence, as though, once initiated, women would delight in more of the same. Certainly "sorrow" more fittingly describes the emotion after rape (and perhaps it more fittingly describes even the state of motherhood). The passage from virginity or from wedded bliss to motherhood is indeed important, but *the rape myth is not truly representative of that passage.*

Other interpretations of the centrality of the rape myth have been offered by Susan Brownmiller, Phyllis Chesler, and R.R. Holt. The last considers it a fascinating possibility that all such myths, legends, or simple fiction which incorporates recognizable images of the primary process may comprise what he calls:

*an indoctrination into consolidated and extended forms*
*of the primary process, a cultural transmission of ways*
*to dream, to fantasy consciously and unconsciously,*
*even to construct delusional systems and other kinds of*
*symptoms, ways that are culturally viable because*
*rooted in certain kinds of world views . . . .* 28

This statement has profound implications: that we learn through myth how to think and to fantasize. Others agree: Phyllis Chesler also believes that myths, particularly the rape myth, can suggest ways for us to dream and to act. According to her, romantic love is psychologically predicated on such a forceful sexual union between Daughter and Father figures. 29 Susan Brownmiller concurs. Citing her own experience with romantic paintings and legends and writing about the female sexual identification within a system of patriarchal myths which highlight such rape, she warns, "The psychic burden under which women function is weighted by a deep belief, borne out by ample evidence, that our attractiveness to men, our sexual desirability, is in direct proportion to our ability to play the victim."[30] Philip Wheelwright correctly suggests that "rape symbolizes one of the most important and emotionally arresting 'passages' in human experience," but the passage is the shift from an innocent belief in one's autonomy to an image of oneself as victim of a brutal force. The passage can be psychologically or physically devastating to both male and female, but the effect on women is particularly debilitating in that their sexual identity is connected to their potential as victim. The Demeter/Persephone myth intertwines several of these strands of "passage."

Demeter, the strong woman who challenges patriarchal law, is offset by Persephone, the woman as victim. The myth portrays the young maiden as a victim of rape, motherhood as consequence of that act, and both mothers as victims of biological processes which deprive them of their maidenhood and inhibit them physically and spiritually. Demeter demands the return of her daughter (who represents both the biological extension of her womanhood and her identity prior to sexual experience); the young maiden rushes to the arms of Demeter (who represents both the mothering she desires in an extended childhood and the motherly role she will assume as part of her sexual identity and as a consequence of her experience). Both the loss and the jubilant return are tinged with sorrow and what the Greeks term *anagnorisis* (recognition, ephiphanic comprehension of identity). The story does not reveal any of the emotions of the maiden. She stands mute, a pawn of forces operating on her.

The new *mythos* emerges in recent portraits of the woman as artist, in the *Künstlerromanen* which focus on the experience of the mother/daughter artist and which allow the daughter to speak. The myth dramatizes the ambivalence attending her sexual identification.

The myth is pertinent to these novels for yet another reason. Structurally, the myth celebrates the origin of a cycle of birth/death/rebirth, supposedly the monomyth of all literature. But in the female version, the cycle is perpetual. Demeter's success is limited; Persephone is doomed to return to Hades. Phyllis Chesler points out that the Eleusinian emotions of catharsis "are rooted in an acceptance of nature and biology's supremacy. . . . The inevitable sacrifice of self that biology demands of women in most societies is at the heart of the Demetrian myth."[31] As a woman, a choice of sacrifices remains the female writer's fate. Obsessed by the necessity to discover alternatives, the female novelist structures her fiction to suggest the inefficacy of any choice. She can repeat the sacrifice of self as woman or the sacrifice of womanhood as self (which, to her, means as artist). The cycle is eternal.

To clarify these statements concerning the relationship, its attendant psychological or emotional forces, and the structure of the novels and the myth, I shall examine some of these mother/daughter-artist connections as they occur in novels of the artist as heroine. Rather than analyze each relationship in each novel as a separate entity, I shall use the myth as a thread to draw together the various strands. By inter-weaving the myth and concrete examples from the novels, I shall indicate the pattern of content, theme, and structure constituting the female version of the *Künstlerroman*.

## MARY OLIVIER: A LIFE

May Sinclair's novel, *Mary Olivier: A Life* (1919), begins with the visions of a very young girl. Having a nightmare after being teased by her father, she remembers her mother comforting her: "Mama's breast: a smooth, cool round thing that hung to your hands and slipped from them when they tried to hold it."[32] The longing to hold on to security, to comfort, to the source of nurture, is clear. However, the young girl is not long allowed such dependency. Because Mary will also develop such breasts, she is trained quickly by her mother to be self-less. "God is grieved every time Mary is self-willed and selfish" (p. 14), she tells her daughter. The brothers' selfishness is excused or praised as aggressiveness. Mary, the only daughter, must be molded to womanhood. An especially bright girl, she innocently questions the logic of adults and their training in an embarrassing way. Both her mother and her nurse show more affection to the boys.

As an adolescent moving biologically from maiden to woman, she experiences violent shifts of emotions toward her mother: "They might at least have told you about the pain. The knives of pain. You had to

50

clench your fists till the fingernails bit into the palms." She throws a hot glance of resentment at her mother: "You had no business to have me. You had no business to have me." She denies one side of her own personality when she feels this antipathy toward her mother: "Somebody else's eyes. Somebody else's thoughts. Not yours. Not yours" (p. 124). But a bit of mothering by Mrs. Olivier brings Mary back from this underworld of hate and pain: "Mama got up and leaned over you and covered you with the rug. . . . Her mouth pushed out to yours, making a small sound like a moan. You heard yourself cry: 'Mamma, Mamma, you are adorable!' That was you" (p. 124). When Mary experiences the pain of menstruation, her mother is able to give her undiluted nurturance. Mary, then, is not a threat; she is, like her mother, a victim of female biology. However, when Mary moves into realms perceived by her mother as masculine, Mrs. Olivier must be harsh and role-train her daughter. The two battle over Mary's rights to the books her brother has left behind. Mary continues to feel ambivalent towards her mother, vacillating between adoration and rejection, between loving and needing to be loved, between mothering and the need to be mothered, depending upon the nature of her acts.

When her father dies, Mary and her mother are thrown together but not united:

> In bed they had turned their backs on each other, and she had the feeling that her mother shrank from her as from somebody unclean who had omitted to wash herself with prayer. She wanted to take her mother in her arms and hold her tight. But she couldn't. She couldn't. (p. 190)

This passage reflects the ambivalence Mary feels about her own body, about mothering, about needing nurturance. It is an example of the dual message which Adrienne Rich claims that each girl receives either explicitly or implicitly through her mother and the cultural institutions which surround them both:

> Throughout patriarchal mythology, dream-symbolism, theology, language, two ideas flow side by side: one, that the female body is impure, corrupt, the site of discharges, bleedings, dangerous to masculinity, a

51

*source of moral and physical contamination, "the devil's gateway." On the other hand, as mother the woman is beneficent, sacred, pure, asexual, nourishing; and the physical potential for motherhood--that same body with its bleedings and mysteries--is her single destiny and justification in life. These two ideas have become deeply internalized in women, even in the most independent of us . . . .* [33]

Mary's mother is transmitting this double-coded message. The Demeter who beckons to the young maiden bears the shadow of the underworld; the maiden who would enfold the mother must do so despite ambivalence about the role her own body will force her to play. In the novel Mary feels the need to mother and to be mothered but cannot overcome her resentment of the double-coded message about her own body as a necessary part of the roles of mother or maiden.

She realizes that approval from her mother requires one of them to change: "To be happy with her either you or she had to be broken, to be helpless and little like a child" (p. 194). In the pure realm of myth, the mother is strong and constant. Persephone is weak and victimized. In order to play Demeter, there must be a Persephone and vice versa. In the real world, the desire to play the strong mother or the maiden child exists in every woman, but the pure mythic counterpart is then necessary.

When Mary finally gets a beau, she thinks immediately of marriage. Being no longer a child and wanting to accept her womanly role, she believes her mother will surely let her marry. Instead, Mrs. Olivier says, " 'I'd rather see you in your coffin' " (p. 210). The connection between marriage and death has been made. The pull between the potential ravisher and the brooding mother has begun. Mary is somehow flattered by this tug of war: "[Mother] hated Maurice Jourdain, yet you felt that in some queer way she loved you because of him" (p. 214). In trying to protect Mary from this man, Mrs. Olivier is behaving as a "good mother"--exhibiting protectiveness which seems related to if not a part of maternal nurturance. Mrs. Olivier explains, " 'I don't want my only daughter to go away and leave me' " (p. 229). Mary responds ambivalently to this protection: "She hated her mother. She adored her and hated her" (p. 229).

Writing poems, Mary gains a measure of happiness, "happiness that was no good to Mamma, no good to anybody but you, secret and selfish; that was your happiness. It was deadly sin" (p. 234). Mary is sensitive to the devouring nature of her mother's love. She protects her inner, secret self which she feels her mother hates: " 'She doesn't *know* she hates me. She never knows that awful sort of thing. And of course she loved me when I was little. She'd love me now if I stayed little . . .'' (p. 249). Again, Mary feels the necessity to play the helpless maiden, Persephone, if she is to receive Demeter's love and protection. She suffers painful, ambivalent feelings about the process of individuation at the expense of her mother's love, which is dependent upon her assuming the proper role. If she sews, for instance, Mary experiences a pleasing glance from Mrs. Olivier: " 'Why do you look at me so kindly when I'm sewing?' '' Mary asks. Then her mother replies, " 'Because I like to see you behaving like a little girl, instead of tearing about and trying to do what boys do' '' (p. 70). The same is true of her writing. Mary feels guilty, selfish, unlovable, for pursuing interests which do not conform to Mrs. Olivier's notion of the female role. Her brother does not experience such rejection when he wishes to become independent.

Whereas her brother could leave in order to establish his manhood, Mary has been groomed to see relationships as taking precedence over her own selfish interests, particularly her art. Mrs. Olivier wants to lose her daughter neither to a man nor to a publisher. If the latter pulls them apart, Mrs. Olivier says, once again, " 'I'd rather see you in your coffin' '' (p. 349). At this point, Mary realizes that she *is* in a coffin of sorts. As an independent artist, Mary would be denying her role as a woman and challenging Mrs. Olivier's sense of responsibility and her definition of womanhood. If Mary does not accept the traditional feminine role, Mrs. Olivier has not raised her daughter successfully. Mary will also be challenging Mrs. Olivier's chosen lifestyle. Whereas each woman needs the emotional sustenance a mother can give, the artist is drawn by an open field and the possibility of pursuing her vision of beauty, independently. For her, the Demeter figure who insists on a return to conventional modes of behavior looms as a Terrible Mother. Wanting to retrieve her daughter from a fate worse than Hades, such a mother consigns her loved one to another form of death--the death of creativity and independence. In such human interplay, both women suffer emotionally. Physical symptoms sometimes hint at such suffering. In this novel, the mother has a slight stroke; the daughter develops a nervous heart condition. Each develops an illness that can force her to play the victim, the young maiden who needs to be rescued by the strong mother figure.* Mary feels divided by her contradictory needs: " 'My body'll stay here and take care of her all my life, but my *self* will have got away . . . . There mayn't be much left when I'm done, but at least it'll be me' " (p. 252). Her brother replies to this comment that she's mad.

She is not insane or schizoid. Instead, she has been programmed to care for others, to play Demeter retrieving children, to play Persephone the victim for the approval of her mother, all as part of her sexual identity. She denies herself for her mother, her brother, and her lover. The happiness she occasionally feels while writing seems sinful to her; a freedom which belongs to a separate being both attracts and repels her: "It was open to you to own it as your self or to detach yourself from it in your horror" (p. 312). The repulsion she feels could be a response either to artistic demons or to the demonic pull of conventions: "The tug of the generations before you, trying to drag you back to them?" (p. 312).

Torn in this tug of war between artistic self and sexual identity, between death in life or life in death, Mary finds an old letter praising her, a teacher's letter her mother had kept from her. A crucial scene develops, one that occurs in most novels of the artist as heroine, the confrontation between mother and daughter. Mrs. Olivier admits that Mary, being different, threatened her:

> *"You weren't like any of the others. I was afraid of you. You used to look at me with your little bright eyes. I felt as if you knew everything I was thinking . . . . I suppose I-I didn't like your being clever. It was the boys I wanted to do things. Not you."*

*Phyllis Chesler theorizes in *Women and Madness* that many of women's illnesses develop from such a need.

> *"Don't-Mamma darling--don't."*
>
> . . . . . . . . . . . . . . . . . . . . . . . . . . . . . . . . . . . . .
>
> *"I was jealous of you, Mary. And I was afraid for my life you'd find it out."* (p. 325)

As a woman who has elected or has been subjected to wife- and mother-hood, Mrs. Olivier has felt bound by the conventions of her role. She too longs for the maiden's seeming potential freedom, which she perceives as a property of the masculine realm. In dreaming of that freedom, she has harshly and ambiguously presented a sexual model, a positional figure, to her daughter. Having partially and personally identified with her mother as a woman, Mary does not want to hear her mother's self-degrading confession, which somewhat demeans any woman; nor does she wish to see her mother, who should in her eyes be the strong Demetrian figure, act as a victim. The pair are tied to one another.

Eventually, Mary meets another man who wants to marry her, but by then she is committed to the welfare of her mother, who has become senile. She tells her lover: " 'You can't leave London because of your work. I can't leave this place because of Mamma. She'd be miserable in London. I can't leave her. She hasn't anybody but me' " (p. 348). Mary has been groomed for motherhood and accepts the Demetrian role, though she never becomes a biological mother. Knowing that the presence of a senile mother-in-law would affect her lover's research and damage his career, she refuses to join him. She also refuses to leave her mother.

Although the stasis of this novel is eventually changed by the death of Mrs. Olivier, Mary remains tied. Eventually overcoming her physical need for the lover who didn't wait, she continues emotionally or spiritually to need her mother: "I'd give anything to have been able to think about her as Mark thought [freely, emotionally, male to female, son to mother, unhampered by crises of sexual identity], to feel about her as he felt. If only I had known what she was really like" (p. 376). The desire to be united with Demeter remains.

Although this novel ostensibly focuses on the development of Mary Olivier as an artist and an individual, the major portion of the novel deals with the interrelationship between mother and daughter, with the latter's need to be joined in spirit to the maternal nurturance which she lacks and which she eventually seeks in a mystical suspension of will that resembles death. The novel mirrors the situation of Demeter/Persephone--the eternal seasonal separation of mother and daughter, of nurturance withheld, of the maiden's forced indoctrination into the world of mothering, of the sorrows that attend the eternal cycle, and the mystical feeling that accompanies the indoctrination into eternity.


## PILGRIMAGE

The heroine of Dorothy Richardson's *Pilgrimage* (1913-1957) exhibits similar longings with similar results. She enters adolescence loathing women in general. For one reason, they always smiled. Even her mother's smile disturbs Miriam, who recalls, "It was the only funny horrid thing about her" (I, 21-22). This heroine sees the smile as an indication of women's positional inferiority and their willing suspension of thought. The smiles cover nervousness, timidity, flattery, ignorance, hypocrisy, and perhaps even rage. The smile represents for Miriam her mother's sexual role, and her attitude toward the smile suggests the ambivalence she has in accepting that role. She begins to identify with her mother's body and with her father's brain. She identifies personally with her mother and positionally with her father. She remembers her mother triumphantly in connection with several days of pain:

> *Bewilderment and pain. . . . her mother's constant presence ....... as she drove with her mother, telling her of pain and she alone in the midst of it . . . for always . . . pride, long moments of deep pride. . . . Eve and Sarah congratulating her, Eve stupid and laughing . . . the new bearing of the servants . . . Lilly Belton's horrible talks fading away to nothing. (I, 137)*

This passage, written vaguely as the heroine's stream of consciousness, seems to describe Miriam's menarche and her mother's discussion of the menses or of childbirth. Even with the attendant pain, Miriam feels proud to have a woman's body and to partake of the womanly heritage. But, despite this rapport with her mother and her willing identification with her mother's body, Miriam rejects her mother as a source of intelligence.

When Miriam is intellectually befuddled, her mother cannot relieve her distress: "She had no reasoning power. She could not help because she did not know" (I, 169). The mother who has lived a life of pain, suffering, and self-abnegation offers only this advice to Miriam as an entry into femininity: " 'Don't go so deeply into everything, chickie. You must learn to take life as it comes' " (I, 169). Miriam grows to believe there is nothing for women in marriage and children if they exclude the world of ideas. After committing herself to obtaining a man, a woman seems doomed to an underworld dead to intellect. Stuck in that Hades, women lose their attractiveness. Miriam states the dilemma: "Their husbands grew to hate them because they had no thoughts. But if a woman had thoughts a man would not be 'silly' with her . . ." (I, 439). If she is to appear feminine, Miriam believes that she must appear brainless. Consequently, she begins to identify positionally with her father's worldliness, his interest in ideas. The relationship clouds her sense of self as woman. Chodorow has commented, about situations like this, "The formation of ego autonomy through identification with and idealization of her father may be at the expense of her positive sense of feminine self." [34]

Vacillating between what she considers to be a masculine realm of intellect and a feminine domain of feeling, Miriam worries that her mother will reject her if she discovers her unconventional life and thoughts. For instance, Miriam begins to smoke. For her, smoking is a defiance of conventional womanhood. Wishing at a party to indicate her distaste for the ingratiating smiles and somewhat hypocritical flattery of the female guests, she begins smoking so they'll know she's a "new woman" of the 1920's who hates their mode of life. Her mother, of course, is not present.

Later, when she is tending her nervous mother, Miriam is rocked by the older woman's forthright outburst:

> *'My life has been so useless,' said Mrs. Henderson*
> *suddenly. Here it was . . . a jolt . . . an awful physical*
> *shock, jarring her body. . . . . . . . . . Mother--almost killed*
> *by things she could not control, having done her duty all*

*her life . . . doing thing after thing had not satisfied her*
*. . . being happy and brave had not satisfied her.*
*There was something she had always wanted, for*
*herself . . . even mother. . . . (I, 472)*

Miriam tries to comfort her mother by insisting that Mrs. Henderson's concern for the world at large was not necessary, that her position as housewife and mother was estimable, and that her life has been worthwhile. Acting motherly and feeling that she is finally conforming to a prepared mold, Miriam thinks: "This was what she had been born for, if only she could hold on. She felt very old. No more happiness . . ." (I, 473). Brought to the world of motherhood, of nurture, of caring, Miriam feels that her free spirit, her maidenhood, is gone. Responding momentarily as she believes a "true woman" would, she nevertheless is repelled by the constant concern which such a role entails. The tension builds. Miriam's mother pleads, " 'I should be better if I could be with you . . .' " Miriam thinks, "oh Lord . . . impossible" but says, " 'You must be with me as much as you like.' " Reacting as a nurturing female, Miriam role-plays in her thoughts: "That was the thing. That was what must be done somehow." But the independent inner self finally acts explosively:

*'Mother! would you mind if I smoke a cigarette?'*

*It was suddenly possible, the unheard-of, unconfessed*
*. . . suddenly easy and possible.*

*'My dearest child,' Mrs. Henderson's flushed face*
*crimsoned unresistingly. She was shocked and ashamed*
*and half delighted. Miriam gazed boldly, admiring and*
*adoring. She felt she had embarked on her first real*
*flirtation . . . . . . . She lit a cigarette with downcast lids and*
*a wicked smile, throwing a triumphant possessive*
*glance at her mother as it drew. The cigarette was*
*divine. It was divine to smoke like this, countenanced*
*and beloved--scandalous and beloved. (I, 474)*

By smoking, Miriam is fleeing from womanhood, at least from the burden of womanhood as she understands it. Karen Horney believed that the motives for such flights generally were guilt and fear.[35] Alfred

Adler suggested that such metaphorical flights occur because there are only two sex roles possible: "One must orient oneself according to one of two models, either that of an ideal woman, or according to that of an ideal man. Desertion from the role of woman can therefore appear only as 'masculine,' and vice versa." [36] Although some might say that Miriam is rejecting the Demeter for the Persephone role, the language suggests otherwise.

The moment with her mother provides an epiphany of sorts for Miriam, but she perceives the communication as that between male and female. To unite woman to woman at this juncture, Miriam would have to assume the role of Demeter and offer unconditional mothering and care. Unwilling to restrict herself so completely, Miriam wants to burst the bonds of womanhood, as she sees it, and identify instead with the male who is free from such restraints. The language hints at this identity crisis. Miriam's embarkment on a "flirtation," her bold gaze, her "triumphant possessive glance" all point to an identification with her father. Only if her mother recovered could they really be "maidens," free spirits, playing by the sea; at least, only then could Miriam remain the unburdened maiden. Adrienne Rich explains the negative feeling that many women develop about "mothering":

> We are, none of us, "either" mothers or daughters; to our amazement, confusion, and greater complexity, we are both. . . . Into the mere notion of "mothering" we may carry, as daughters, negative echoes of our own mothers' martyrdom, the burden of their valiant, necessarily limited efforts on our behalf, the confusion of their double messages. But it is a timidity of the imagination which urges that we can be "daughters" --therefore free spirits--rather than "mothers"--defined as eternal givers. [37]

Wanting to be either the ravishing male who whisks her mother away or the asexual, free-spirited maiden prior to abduction, Miriam is left instead with the burdensome role of attendant. Eventually awakened by a lurching in the night, Miriam realizes that her mother has gone mad, "the best, gentlest thing she knew in the world, openly despairing at last" (I, 488). After what is suggestively described as her mother's suicide, Miriam feels bereft: "There was no one in the world who would care if she never appeared anywhere again. She sat shrinking before this truth. ....... She wondered that she had never put it to herself before. It must always have been there since her mother's death" (II, 326). She realizes that her need for maternal nurturance will never be filled. Unable to assume the role of Demeter, Miriam forever loses the role of Persephone. Often disoriented, she repeatedly finds herself near a group of shops which had special significance to her mother. For a while, Miriam believes that such disorientation may indicate that she, too, will become a madwoman (thereby identifying, positionally, with her mother).

Considering herself an anomaly, Miriam thereafter rejects the role of either maiden or mother. In an argument with a man whose intellect she enjoys, she claims that "women never have been subject" and that feminists who fight for emancipation "are not only an insult to woman-hood. They are a libel on the universe" (III, 218, 220). Her reasons for arguing in this vein are complex.

First of all, she is a woman. As such, she is a part in a chain which she nevertheless does not want connected with bondage. She must alternately deny woman's bondage or her own womanhood. She asks, " 'You think I can cheerfully regard myself as an emancipated slave, with traditions of slavery for memory and the form of a slave as an everlasting heritage?' " (III, 220). When the man says that heredity is cross-wise and that she is probably more the daughter of her father, she rejects the role, saying, "If anything, I am my mother's son" (III, 220). The man immediately counters with the statement that women's desire for sons indicates the dissatisfaction of women with their role and a consequent need to change society so they can more easily enter a man's world. Miriam argues:

> 'That is another question. She [such a woman] hopes they will give her the understanding she never had from their father. In that I am my mother's son for ever. If there's a future life, all I care for is to meet her. If I could have her back for ten minutes I would gladly give up the rest of my life. . . . ' (III, 220)

Miriam still shows her need for maternal nurturance, even while she demands independence. In her mind, both are male prerogatives, so she insists that she is masculine.

She also identifies with men because she perceives as unwomanly her interests in philosophy and serious writing. She claims that such manly fields are less creative, actually, than womanly arts of hostessing and creating atmospheres. Miriam insists that what women need is homage for these arts and for their sensitivity and tact. They have been put on pedestals for their beauty and their potential as breeders, but they have not been given credit for their special talents and abilities, such as those her mother had.

Although Miriam does not want to be confined in a temple of domesticity, she acknowledges the value of a matrifocal standard of achievements and a Demetrian concern for relationships. Because she and her mother were not united, not even for two-thirds of the year, Miriam rejects the role of woman and feels herself forever separated from the figure of Demeter. Adrienne Rich comments on such rejection:

> *Few women growing up in patriarchal society can feel mothered enough; the power of our mothers, whatever their love for us and their struggles on our behalf, is too restricted. And it is the mother through whom patriarchy early teaches the small female her proper expectations. The anxious pressure of one female on another to conform to a degrading and dispiriting role can hardly be termed "mothering," even if she does this believing it will help her daughter to survive.*
>
> *Many daughters live in rage at their mothers for having accepted, too readily and passively, "whatever comes."*
> *A mother's victimization does not merely humiliate her, it mutilates the daughter who watches her for clues as to what it means to be a woman.* [38]

Consequently, like Miriam, a woman can grow up thinking of herself as masculine, or she can, from an insecurity about her identity in general, develop a lifelong need for approval.

## A WOMAN OF GENIUS

Olivia, the narrator of Mary Austin's *A Woman of Genius* (1912), grows in the latter direction. Austin clearly spells out the nature of that need in the words of her heroine:

> *I seem to have been born into the knowledge that*
> *the breast, the lap, and the brooding tenderness were*
> *the sole prerogative of babies; it was imperative to*
> *your larger estate not to exhibit the weakness of*
> *wanting them.* 39

Despite this intellectual comprehension, her body exhibits its need. Olivia describes the feeling she has, watching her mother rock the latest baby:

> *. . . all at once, I knew, with what certainty it hurts me*
> *still to remember, how it felt to be held so close . . .*
> *close . . . and safe . . . and the smell of the breast . . . . . . .\**
> *knew it as if I had been but that moment dispossessed*
> *. . . and the need . . . as I know now I have always*
> *needed to be so enfolded. (p. 20)*

Crying hysterically yet trying to work her way through the need and to develop her independence, she is shaken by her mother's hand: ''I was struggling desperately to get away from it . . . away from the mother, who held me so to the mother I had just remembered . . .'' (p. 21). That Olivia now understands her ambivalence is obvious. Nevertheless, the need to be mothered constantly returns.

Though she loves her mother in this very passionate, almost sexual way, she has difficulty identifying with her. Olivia's need for mothering and her sexual identification with her mother as a woman conflict with her opinion of herself as an artist. As the narrator explains, ''Though I have often heard my mother spoken of as one of the best women in the world, she was the last to have provided me with a definite pattern of behavior'' (p. 44). In a woman, talent and the need for mothering--the need for approval from the mother who is fashioning the daughter for a sexual role she expects her to fill--clash so violently that the genius may

---

\*Single-spaced ellipses will indicate my deletions from the stream-of-consciousness text.

feel cut off from human affections. Robert Seidenberg comments about this conflict between identity and self-attainment:

> *If a girl in her development has no other than the image of a woman in the domestic role, this image will be internalized and become her principal knowledge of what a woman is and does. . . . In spite of later worldly education, the earliest lessons come from all-powerful, life-giving and sustaining giants--parents--and they stick. This learning is, then, the education of how to please, how to be loved, how to survive.* [40]

Seidenberg is not suggesting that a woman will never grow in other directions from her mother, but that the internal image is affected.

Because Olivia sees herself as a cuckoo dropped in her mother's nest, she searches for affection elsewhere. Indeed, she develops that lifelong need for approval. She admits, "I was in love all the time, I didn't know with whom, but always wanting somebody . . . trying to get through to something; trying to mate" (p. 290). Because monetary status and approval are so welded, Olivia almost becomes a kept woman, "put at a disadvantage, not by a monetary obligation," she explains, "so much as by the inevitable feminine reaction toward the source of care and protection" (p. 364).

The narrator eventually experiences a temporary illicit passion because she doesn't want to leave the stage and her lover does not consider the atmosphere right for his two girls, whom he wants raised "nicely." The condition her lover requires resembles her former husband's demand, "not of loving and being faithful, but of living over the store" (p. 246). Both men insist on a prescribed lifestyle. Both would have her play the nurturing role.

If she chose the domestic role, Olivia would be rewarded not only by her future second husband's money and status but, strangely enough, by the sympathy and approval of her mother, who understands the connection between marriage and position, who can comprehend the sacrifices necessary in such a marriage, but who cannot approve of her daughter's life on the stage. The narrator can only fall back on the knowledge that loving is not wrong for the artist, but "living in one place and by a particular pattern . . . thinking that *because* you are married you have to leave off this and take up that which you wouldn't think of doing for any other reason" (p. 505). Marriage, removed to such a place, is for Olivia a physical and psychological rape and such an existence is, like living in Hades, impossible. The novel ends with Olivia being offered this Hades of marriage and the haven of a conditional motherly love which depends on her isolation in that hellish realm. She chooses to reject the warmth of such encircling arms and to remain on stage where she can play roles for the artificial, loveless, but less restricting, approval of the audience.

## CATHERINE CARTER

Whereas Olivia rejects her mother's lifestyle yet exhibits anger at the end of the novel because she is unable to cathect intense and related needs to give and to receive nurturance, the heroines of Pamela Johnson's *Catherine Carter* (1968) and of Willa Cather's *The Song of the Lark* (1915) experience an epiphany involving their art and their mothers which allows them gladly to sacrifice a portion of their lives for their art. In the novels previously examined, the mothers were "family-centered" and committed to develop such a focus in their daughters. But even when the mother promotes a different lifestyle, the tension is not much relieved, for the relationship is still circumscribed by twin needs to identify with sex-role figures and to receive love, both of which sometimes conflict with the artist's need to establish her own identity.

In Pamela Johnson's novel, *Catherine Carter*, the heroine's relationship to her mother is immediately suggested by the first-page reference to the older woman as "The Little General." She is a commander, a widow who meddles in her daughter's life, a woman who constantly grieves for her deceased husband, and a stage-mother who dominates, orders, promotes her daughter, and praises her in a loud and embarrassing fashion. Ashamed of her, Catherine can neither reject her nor abandon the goal Mrs. Carter wants her to reach.

Searching for a love less dependent upon her stage success, Catherine falls for the questionable charms of Malcolm Rivers. She marries him and develops a sexual appetite which he has no desire to slake. She receives little help from Mrs. Carter about this predicament, who admits in Victorian fashion, "It [intercourse] was never agreeable to *me*. Of course it is not agreeable to any woman, except those of a certain class . . . ." [41] The conversation obviously does not bridge but widens the gap between mother and daughter:

> *Catherine looked at her across the wastes dividing*
> *them. How could her mother ever understand her?*
> *Marriage had taught Catherine that the drive of her love*
> *was as strong in her body as in her imagination. She*
> *knew the cyclical tide of desire, the tenderness, the*
> *hunger, the longing to be borne down by a passion as*
> *strong as her own. (p. 219)*

There are two ways to interpret this passage: Catherine may be exhibiting a healthy sexual drive which seeks a suitable outlet. Or, her intense need may suggest a lack of nurturance which erupts as a search for the mother who will save her (Demeter) or the god who will ravish her (Pluto). Although modern women admit sexual drive, their sexual needs are not easily interpreted, as Freud well knew. Bardwick explains the confusion:

> *The psychoanalytic idea that women are moved by*
> *strong sexual drives in the same way that men are has*
> *led to the overestimation of sex as a significant variable*
> *in the lives of women. There has also been a lack of*
> *recognition of the cyclic nature of desire and of the*
> *strength of maternity-nurturance as a powerful female*
> *need.* [42]

The man Catherine eventually chooses as her second husband is older, protective, nurturing, and physically responsive to her needs. By contrast, Mrs. Carter, in trying to save her maiden from the ugliness of sexuality, can suggest only that her daughter think of something else during intercourse. Catherine remains frustrated at this point by a husband who does not love her, a lover who will not make love to her because he respects her, and a mother who conditions love on her daughter's remaining respectable and artistically successful.

Wanting to be pursued by Henry Peverel, Catherine flees to Venice. Mrs. Carter stands by, feeling as helpless as a child, since she is not called to rescue her maiden daughter. Henry Peverel eventually wins Catherine in marriage. Although the novel centers on professional rivalry and resolution of their love affair, the denouement depends upon the crescendo and climax in the tension between mother and daughter. Both resolutions depend upon Catherine's successfully playing the strong role of Cleopatra opposite Peverel's Antony.

When Henry finally allows Catherine to play Cleopatra, she feels inadequate while rehearsing the role. There is one line she cannot intone correctly, a line Mrs. Carter helps her to interpret. The mother explains the relief she got from turning her husband's room into a shrine and pretending that he wasn't dead. She says, "It didn't seem like a parade of grief to me" (p. 492). The comment helps Catherine perform brilliantly as Cleopatra and to execute a powerful crescendo of feeling when she cries, " 'I am again for Cydnus / To meet Mark Antony!' " (p. 498).

Although she still needs her husband's approval for the job well done, Catherine is able to move into womanhood with assurance through her mother's help. Both mother and daughter are united by the mother's interpretation. The mother is able to feel pride in and a part of her daughter's success as an actress. The daughter is able to take pride in her womanhood, her heritage, as a result. The mother boasts:

> *'To think I should have had a* clever *notion!'* . . .
> *'But perhaps you got some of your brains from me.*
> *Did Henry ever say so? Herbert was artistic, but I'm*
> *sure it's not all his doing. I used to write quite original*
> *compositions when I was a girl.'* (p. 493)

Demeter (Mrs. Carter) and Persephone (Catherine) are united, despite Catherine's emotional attachment to Henry. The epiphany of their union resolves the tensions and conflicts which begin the novel. However, this happy ending avoids some of the problems of real life (Catherine miscarries a baby girl who might have created new tensions; Catherine's success depends to some extent upon her beauty, which will fade; her lover/husband is several years her senior and the age difference may eventually cause problems).

66

Whereas this happy ending seems a bit "stagey," the epiphany in *The Song of the Lark* contributes to the stage success of the heroine without straining one's willing suspension of disbelief. Thea Kronborg's mother is also a strong figure, but a practical household administrator who establishes priorities in her dominion. Usually, the first priority is the latest baby. Despite Mrs. Kronborg's unconscious dignity and her noble carriage, she is somewhat harried by the many children she has. Consequently, Thea does not receive much individual attention. Despite needing the love and approval of her mother, Thea comes to realize that her family ties must be severed. "Her mother was all right, but her mother was a part of the family [and its jealousies and squabbles], and she was not. In the nature of things, her mother had to be on both sides" (p. 301). The small house promotes intimacy and a family togetherness which does not mesh with the artist's need to develop her own individuality.

She eventually reaches the Cliff-Dweller ruins, a place where she can leave "the stream of meaningless activity and undirected effort" (p. 373). Getting back to primal sources of Indian women, she identifies with them as mothers and nourishes herself on their spirit, their art, their pottery. She feels a kindred spirit and an obligation to do her best. Adrienne Rich has eloquently described the benefits of such an identification:

> For centuries, daughters have been strengthened and energized by nonbiological mothers, who have combined a care for the practical values of survival with an incitement toward further horizons, a compassion for vulnerability with an insistence on our buried strengths. [43]

Thea bathes in the stream of her Indian foremothers and recognizes the connection between the stream, the broken pottery, and art: "What was any art but an effort to make a sheath, a mould in which to imprison for a moment the shining, elusive element which is life itself . . ." (p. 378). Whereas her own mother presented her with a picture of womanhood steeped in domesticity and procreativity but somewhat removed from creativity, the mental image of the Indian women who had the artistic and magical power to transform clay into pottery and to create a beautiful and a practical pot stirs Thea to reach her ideal.

From this spiritual union with strong female artists of ancient times, Thea absorbs the power and simplicity of early Indian Earth Mothers: "She felt united and strong" (p. 380). At that moment she tosses away any positional obligations to her biological parents and strikes off on her own. Despite later momentary needs to nestle in peace with her family, she does not succumb. The artist in Thea feels restricted by Mrs. Kronborg, despite the encouragement offered. Thea admires and identifies with her mother personally but must reject her, positionally, in order to reach perfection in art.

Cather justifies Thea's rejection of her mother's role, to some extent, by a description of that role as empty in the long run. Mrs. Kronborg complains, late in life, that the bright ones get away to make their own life: "Seems like the brighter they are, the farther they go" (p. 492).

In Cather's novel, Mrs. Kronborg dies while separated from her favorite daughter. Thea refuses to return because, to her, performing a role on stage is more important than playing the role of daughter to a dying mother. However, Thea is able to unite her ideal of art and her personal admiration for her mother in a particularly difficult Wagnerian role. Fricka, the character, is usually portrayed as a nagging wife. By performing this role as a tribute to her mother, Thea transforms it: Fricka's "reproaches to *Wotan* were the pleadings of a tempered mind, a consistent sense of beauty" (p. 539). Although Thea is able to capture the essence of her mother, she cannot have the comfort of her mother's presence. She must remain separated from family ties.

Thea endures the loneliness of life on stage by learning from her Indian mothers "the inevitable hardness of human life" (p. 554), a lesson evident, as well, in the Demeter/Persephone myth. Understanding the sacrifices made by the Indian pottery makers, by her own mother, and by herself as an artist helps her to transform the Wagnerian role of the hen-pecking bitch into a mythical figure of strength. Using matrifocal insights, she transmutes a patriarchal image of woman and gains nobility for herself, at least on stage. The sorrow and compassion she depicts there echo the sorrow and compassion dramatized in the myth of the lost Persephone. However, this Persephone dares not return to Demeter for fear of absorption in the mother/daughter cycle. Each woman suffers a loss in the separation.

## TO THE LIGHTHOUSE

Despite the sorrow which surrounds her, the Greek Demeter is a strong if not an inviolate figure. A twentieth-century character who also projects such mythic power is Mrs. Ramsay in Virginia Woolf's *To the Lighthouse* (1927). Seeing this resemblance, Joseph Blotner calls Mrs. Ramsay "almost an incarnation of Demeter."[44] There is a resemblance, but in this novel, the unique focus is significant.

In the Greek myth only two places are open to Persephone when her maidenhood is violated. She is wife/mother in Hades or daughter/mother in Eleusis. The audience discovers nothing about a self outside these roles, neither from the narrator nor from Persephone's own statements. *To the Lighthouse* may be viewed as a twentieth-century retelling of the myth by an author who is interested in the psyche of both Demeter and Persephone. Though the narrator is an objective observer, inobtrusively omniscient, much of the novel, especially the last chapter, filters through the eyes of Lily, an artist who stands outside mother, wife, and even daughter roles, who threatens her own identity by rejecting them, and who tries instead to nourish via her art.

Mrs. Ramsay is a goddess--a Good Mother who is reverenced,[45] compassionate (p. 26), charitable (p. 18), beautiful (p. 25), and intuitive (p. 46). She is also a Terrible Mother who is severe (p. 14), vain (p. 65), high-handed (pp. 73, 75), willful, commanding (p. 76), stern (p. 97), short-sighted (p. 109), frightening (p. 152), and perhaps heartless in her own way (p. 185). In both aspects, she is irresistible (p. 152).

As a powerful mother figure, Mrs. Ramsay can relate only to Lily the independent and as yet unravished maiden, not to Lily the artist. Mrs. Ramsay scorns modern artists in general (p. 23), cares "not a fig" for Lily's painting (p. 77), and insists that "an unmarried woman has missed the best of life" (p. 77). To counteract such a powerful influence, Lily urges "her own exemption from the universal law" (p. 77). The novel, in effect, becomes Persephone's plea for exemption from the eternal cycle of dominance by either Pluto or Demeter.

69

Lily has two strong desires--to paint and to unite with Mrs. Ramsay, who is the quintessence of good and bad maternal nurturance. While with the Ramsays, Lily is "made to feel violently two opposite things at the same time" (p. 154). The woman within wants to be united with Mrs. Ramsay as miraculously and completely as Persephone is re-united with Demeter. Lily openly voices this desire: "Could loving, as people called it, make her and Mrs. Ramsay one? for it was not knowledge but unity that she desired, not inscriptions on tablets, nothing that could be written in any language known to men, but intimacy itself . . ." (p. 79). Whereas Lily the woman wants to be intimately joined with the eternal mother, Lily the artist wishes to remain independent, asexual, in the field, admiring the *narcissus poeticus.*

True, artists of either sex often feel divided by contradictory wishes--to participate fully in the business of life and to separate from this hubbub in order freely to follow their artistic bent. But Lily's wish is more specific; she wants *unity* with Mrs. Ramsay, a desire symptomatic of her intense needs for maternal nurturance and for some assurance of her wholesomeness through sexual identification with the mother figure.

Her relationships with men also revolve around the issues of nur-turance, sexual identity, and artistic independence. Mr. Bankes, a bit older than she, nevertheless represents a possibility for marriage. But the emotion he offers is reverence, "distilled and filtered" (p. 73), the reverence he has for Mrs. Ramsay in particular and womanhood in general; his capacity for physical intimacy with Lily the artist seems limited. Mr. Carmichael represents the male counterpart of Lily's independent, artistic spirit; the man is not won over by Mrs. Ramsay's mothering. Mr. Ramsay represents the intellectual; practical yet demanding of sympathy, he epitomizes the male force that feeds off women's energy. Charles Tansley exemplifies the patriarchal order which both thunders and whispers, "Women can't write, women can't paint" (p. 130). These men force Lily to compare herself to Mrs. Ramsay as a woman and foster doubts about her role as an artist. The polar issues of Lily's sexual identity and her artistic independence are resolved only in an artistic vision.

In life, Lily remains torn by conflicting needs. Because she wants to paint rather than nurture, she sees herself as "not a woman" (p. 226).

Her refusal to spend energy oozing sympathy for others she perceives as "immensely to her discredit, sexually" (p. 228). Choosing to channel her energies into art, she loses a sense of her womanhood. Both men and women must be "drawn out of living, out of community with people" (p. 236) when they paint. But Lily's self-image depends on her identification with the ideal woman, Mrs. Ramsay, who is very much aware of people, things, and the atmosphere surrounding them.

If Lily acts womanly by trying to copy Mrs. Ramsay's behavioral model, she will suffer "dilution" (p. 154), spending too much of her time nurturing others. Consequently, Lily sets her canvas as a barrier to ward off human relations that demand giving, giving, giving (p. 223).

Mrs. Ramsay's death disturbs Lily for two reasons: As a living goddess, she could have provided Lily and others with the nurture they need. Secondly, Lily blames Mrs. Ramsay for the example she has set. To identify with her is to assume her sexual role as well, to feel responsibility toward Mr. Ramsay, to waste time "always trying to bring up some feeling she had not got" (p. 224), and, consequently, to play at painting rather than to deal wholeheartedly with her deadly enemy, the empty canvas. Both the art of painting and the art of mothering demand self-surrender (p. 224). Lily weighs the sacrifice of each art form, her own painting against Mrs. Ramsay's talent for bringing things and people together.

Both art forms erupt as creative fountains. Mrs. Ramsay's sympathetic nature is described as the "fountain and spray of life" at which "the beak of brass, the arid scimitar of the male" (pp. 58-59) can quench its thirst. When Lily paints, forgotten scenes or emotions stored in her unconscious erupt on the canvas "like a fountain spurting over that glaring, hideously difficult white space" (p. 238). The difference between the two fountains is the admiration they receive. Men and women worship Mrs. Ramsay in her role of mother goddess, whereas they denigrate this female artist, an unmarried woman, for trying to paint. Even Mrs. Ramsay comments about Lily, "One could not take her painting very seriously" (p. 29). Mr. Tansley's patriarchal remark demeans all women artists. Whereas the praise and worship Mrs. Ramsay receives replenish the source of her fountain of creative sympathy, Lily remains unnourished, unless she submits to Mrs. Ramsay's control or plays the motherly role. When Lily paints, she challenges not only space, line, and color, but a tradition that would strip her sexual identity unless she fills the Demeter/Persephone mold.

In *To the Lighthouse* a long passage intertwines issues of identity, art, and the need for nurturance and suggests that these concerns may affect the quality of Lily's art or of all women's:

> *Always (it was in her nature, or in her sex, she did not know which) before she exchanged the fluidity of life for the concentration of painting she had a few moments of nakedness when she seemed like an unborn soul, a soul reft of body, hesitating on some windy pinnacle and exposed without protection to all the blasts of doubt. Why then did she do it? . . . What was the good of doing it then, and she heard some voice saying she couldn't paint, saying she couldn't create, as if she were caught up in one of those habitual currents in which after a certain time experience forms in the mind, so that one repeats words without being aware any longer who originally spoke them.*
>
> *Can't paint, can't write, she murmured monotonously, anxiously considering what her plan of attack should be. (pp. 236-37)*

Several different issues and images coalesce in this passage.

For instance, the image she has of herself, isolated, standing on some windy pinnacle, exposed without protection, resembles the one of Mr. Ramsay, who appears "as a stake driven into the bed of a channel . . . marking the channel out there in the floods alone" (p. 69). The position is that of a male guardian. When he arrives at the island of the lighthouse, he seems to Cam to be "leaping into space" (p. 308), daring enough to perish alone. When Lily works at her painting, she feels vulnerable and wonders if life "all was miracle, and leaping from the pinnacle of a tower into the air?" (p. 268). The language suggests the similarity of Mr. Ramsay and Lily as independent spirits. Whereas the male figure seems confident, the female artist does not. Mr. Ramsay does not hesitate to insist on support and attention from women. Indeed, he demands and receives sympathetic boosts of different sorts from Mrs. Ramsay, Lily, and Cam. Lily needs such support, begs for it from Mrs. Ramsay, but detests her own yearning. Long after realizing that she escaped "by the skin of her teeth" from the power of Mrs. Ramsay, Lily feels the need for her return: " 'Mrs. Ramsay! Mrs. Ramsay!' she cried, feeling the old horror come back--to want and want and not to have. Could she inflict that still?" (p. 300). For Lily, the need for nurturance is too closely tied to an identification with the mother figure and to subsequent loss of independence.

Elsewhere in the passage quoted above, Lily describes herself as being "reft of body." The comment suggests that she identifies herself as neither male nor female, but pure asexual spirit. She also says she's "unborn." The term suggests that she feels unmothered. Her feeling of being "exposed without protection" may derive from an awareness that she lacks male protection, a force she could depend upon if she adopted the standard sexual role. In addition, she is "naked," vulnerable to attack, without armor, and stripped of any heritage of helpful female models or writers. Like many artists, she feels the need to be reborn, to create her own identity outside this restrictive tradition. The difference in her case is that she must identify with a male spirit of independence and work in a realm designated as masculine. The self doubt she has about her ability to operate in such a realm makes her anxious. If she transfers that anxiety to the painting, it may, indeed, then be fit only for attics or for destruction.

By writing this passage, Virginia Woolf implicitly raises some questions: Is the inadequacy of the work pre-ordained because women can't paint, can't write? Does the statement, carried in women's unconscious, affect the quality of their work? Does their need to identify with the mother figure affect the seriousness or the quality of their work? Do they lessen their chances for producing great art by identifying positionally with male intellect, drive, independence, and then identifying personally or sexually with breeders of children, sympathetic women who "can't write, can't paint"?

What Lily tries to achieve in her painting is "that razor edge of balance between opposite forces; Mr. Ramsay and the picture" (p. 287). What that opposition represents and what she does achieve are debatable. [46] To me, the picture represents her *womanly* offering to the patriarchal world; it is a discharge of bodily emotions welling from the mother/

daughter cathexis, a fountain of feeling which includes pain, sorrow, and compassion for separation from the source of sustenance, a sorrow which she feels and a compassion which she can offer in turn to males like Mr. Ramsay.

Many critics see that the picture represents an attempt to balance opposite forces. Some see it as an indication of Virginia Woolf's androgynous mind. [47] But Lily views the picture as a force in opposition to Mr. Ramsay. If the latter represents the male principle, the picture itself should represent the feminine offering that balances it.

The painting represents a womanly creation emanating from the mother/daughter cathexis. Though Lily feels removed from Mrs. Ramsay's influence of power, she experiences again and again "the physical sensations that went with the bare look of the steps" (pp. 265-66). Her cries, evoked by the pain of separation, echo Persephone's cries for her mother. The repeated return of Lily's sorrowful sensations also resembles the recurring Persephone/ Demeter separation. Virginia Woolf describes Lily's sensations: "the pain of the want, and the bitter anger (to be called back, just as she thought she would never feel sorrow for Mrs. Ramsay again . . ." (p. 269). Fearful of being inundated by these emotions and her intense identification with Mrs. Ramsay, Lily the artist is "moved . . . by some instinctive need of distance" (p. 270). This need sends her to look for Mr. Ramsay's boat. She bounces back and forth between the father figure and the mother's influence, much as Persephone makes her seasonal travels. Having envisioned Mrs. Ramsay sitting in the chair and casting a shadow on the step, Lily rushes to see Mr. Ramsay "as if she had something she must share" (p. 300). Her need to identify with the behavior of Mrs. Ramsay seems obvious. "Driven by the discomfort of the sympathy which she held undischarged" (p. 241), she seeks Mr. Ramsay, makes connections between Mr. and Mrs. Ramsay and between herself and Mr. and Mrs. Ramsay, and eventually finishes this "attempt at something" (p. 309), a communication of "one's body feeling, not one's mind" (p. 265). When Ramsay has landed at the lighthouse, she feels relieved to have "given him at last" (p. 309) something she wanted him to have. Only then, with the steps again empty, can she draw in the center of the canvas the line which completes her vision.

By trying to make connections, Lily can identity with Mrs. Ramsay, particularly her attempt to unite the people at dinner: "The whole of the effort of merging and flowing and creating rested on her. Again she felt, as a fact without hostility, the sterility of men" (p. 126). With her painting, Lily tries to erase the sterility in her life, which resembles Mr. Carmichael's more than Mrs. Ramsay's. She compares Mrs. Ramsay's bringing people together, "making of the moment something permanent" (p. 241), to her own attempts in art. Instead of working in the fluidity of life, Lily concentrates on the rhythm of strokes on canvas, where "down in the hollow of one wave she saw the next wave towering higher and higher above her" (p. 236). To her, the challenge of the hostile white canvas is as great as the challenge Mrs. Ramsay faces against life, which is "like a wave which bore one up with it and threw one down with it" (p. 73), "terrible, hostile, and quick to pounce on you if you gave it a chance" (p. 92).

This comparison is more than just the usual one of life and art. Virginia Woolf's use of the same wave imagery indicates Lily's need to think of herself in a womanly or acceptable way, to identify with the life-giving forces of Mrs. Ramsay.

Lily still reacts to Charles's remark:

> *Women can't write, women can't paint--what did that matter coming from him, since clearly it was not true to him but for some reason helpful to him, and that was why he said it? Why did her whole being bow, like corn under a wind, and erect itself again from this abasement only with a great and rather painful effort? She must make it once more.* (p. 130)

Ten years later, the painting is an attempt once again to erect herself from this abasement. By identifying with the worshipped Mrs. Ramsay's fight with life, Lily can remove herself somewhat from the stigma of sterility. Whereas Mrs. Ramsay, the female artist of human relations, receives reverence and love, and whereas Mr. Carmichael, the male artist of poetry, receives accolades, the female artist is "a peevish, ill-tempered, dried-up old maid" (p. 226) who sees her own work as "virginal" (p. 77) when measured against Mrs. Ramsay's life and whose work is considered by others as androgynous or sterile. Each time she begins to paint, she feels forced upon herself "her own inadequacy, her insignificance" (p. 32) both as a woman and as an artist. If she offers sympathy directly, she will be caught in the flow of human emotions and will have neither time nor energy to communicate via art. Instead, she tries to make connections via her paint, to divert onto the canvas before her the flood of grief, the "insatiable hunger for sympathy" (p. 226) which both she and Mr. Ramsay feel.

Despite the fact that as she paints, she attempts to subdue "all her impressions as a woman to something much more general" (p. 82), Lily reveals her womanhood, her heritage of Demeter/Persephone, in her art. Lily perceives the canvas as her armor against human relationships that would drain her; nevertheless, on that canvas she can effectively reduce her emotions pertaining to mother and child to "a purple shadow without irreverence" (p. 81). By so doing, she cathects her intense need for nurturance and approval, identifies with Mrs. Ramsay as a woman, and offers this art in compassion for the separation and loss all persons experience.


## THE STORY OF AVIS

Whereas Lily's painting may be symbolic of the nurturing and creative urges of its artist, the painting featured in *The Story of Avis* (1879) represents the sacrifice of a female artist who tries to fulfill the Demetrian role of maternal woman. In this novel Elizabeth Stuart Phelps [Ward] depicts a brilliant young artist, Avis Dobell, who receives critical acclaim before marrying Philip Ostrander. Entering the web of this sexual relationship, Avis is enmeshed therein.

Her entrapment is suggested by the image of a harbor light, whose glow attracts birds during rough weather:

> *Slowly at first, with her head bent, as if she resisted some opposing pressure, then swiftly, as if she had been drawn by irresistible forces, then blindly, like the bird to the light-house, she passed the length of the silent room, and put both hands, the palms pressed together as if they had been manacled, into his.* 48

Soon after marriage, she becomes a mother. Motherhood is shocking to her artistic temperament. Having a delicate, ailing baby who cries a great deal unnerves her. Admitting that she would like relief from the constant care, she must respond to her husband's queries:

> *"Why, Avis," said her husband, "Don't you care-- don't you feel any maternal affection for the little thing?"*
>
> *"No," cried every quavering nerve in the honest young mother; "not a bit!"*
>
> *Perhaps, indeed, she was lacking in what is called the maternal passion as distinct from the maternal devotion. She was perfectly conscious of being obliged to learn to love her baby like anybody else . . . . (p. 274)*

Phelps suggests that a female may naturally feel compelled to give maternal care, but that maternal passion--a love of doing so--must be developed, at least in some mothers.

The problem may lie in Avis's upbringing. Because her mother died when she was young, she lacks a mother's warm affection. She may identify instead with her father's form of striving. Or, she may simply lack training in the nurturance of others:

> *Avis had never lived in the house with a baby; neither had Ostrander. Their vague ideas of the main characteristics of infancy were drawn as, I think I may safely say, those of most young men and women are at the time of marriage, chiefly from novels and romances, in which parentage is represented as a blindly deifying privilege, which it were an irreverence to associate with teething, the midnight colic, or an insufficient income. (p. 275)*

Phelps here suggests the effect literature has on the development of our concepts of life. Fictional ideals rather than the reality of descendental details structure images of the parent-child relationship. The artist has particular difficulty adjusting to the difference between the ideal and the reality.

77

Painting and caring for her baby prove difficult for Avis. Although she completes her major work, the portrait of a sphinx, before the birth of this child, she is not satisfied with the painting's composition. It sits on the easel, awaiting her finishing touch.

Avis gives birth to another child, and one month later receives word that her husband will be fired. When this baby cries, Avis looks at her new "woman-child" and sympathizes: "It seemed to her just then more than she could bear, to know that she had given life to another woman" (p. 319). The compassion she has developed over the long months is tied to self-pity and knowledge of the burdens a woman assumes with housekeeping and motherhood. These duties drag on Avis's spirit: "The child's voice and his father's chimed together oddly. She stood apart from them,--these two intensely wrought male personalities, with whose clamorous selfism it was impossible to reason" (p. 320). Avis fears that her daughter will have to assume the burden of waiting on men like these. She knows that the frail and free-spirited Persephone must change with motherhood into the strong and nurturing woman. Avis's own Demetrian strength and determination seem almost manly. Phelps explains the transformation:

> *So gentle had been the stages by which her great passion had grown into a mournful compassion, her divine ideal become this unheroic human reality, the king of her heart become the dependent on its care,--so quietly this had come about, that, in the first distinct recognition of it all, she felt no shock; only a stern, sad strain upon the muscle of her nature. There was, indeed, a certain manhood in her--it is latent in every woman, and assumes various forms. Avis possessed it only in a differing degree, not in kind, from most other women,--an instinct of strength, or an impulse of protection, which lent its shoulders spontaneously to the increasing individuality of her burden. (pp. 324-25)*

After the arrival of her second child, the dismissal of her husband from his professorship, his infidelity, and his physical collapse, Avis, with a motherly concern for her family's needs, rushes to complete her painting of the sphinx, so that she can sell it. On the canvas, she inserts an "Arab child looking at the Sphinx with his finger on his lips,

78

swearing her to silence . . ." (p. 373). The gesture suggests the stultification Avis has experienced in her roles as housekeeper, mother, and wife. As Phelps explains, in direct author-to-reader style:

> *Women understand--only women altogether--what a dreary will-o-the-wisp is this old, common, I had almost said commonplace, experience, "When the fall sewing is done," "When the baby can walk," "When house-cleaning is over," "When the company has gone," "When we have got through with the whooping-cough," "When I am a little stronger," then I will write the poem, or learn the language, or study the great charity, or master the symphony; then I will act, dare, dream, become. (pp. 272-73)*

After her brief spurt of activity on the Sphinx's portrait, Avis feels immensely burdened, physically and psychologically, by these mundane details. They exile her from the studio:

> *She could not abandon herself to it without a feminine sense of guilt, under which women less tender may thrive callously . . . . She was stunned to find how her aspiration had emaciated during her married life. Household care had fed upon it like a disease. (p. 375)*

When Avis falls ill with diphtheria, Philip has to placate their fretful baby girl and control their son. The confusion is too much for him; he vows to get a nurse. Since the family is already in debt, Avis does not ask him to care for the babies again. She feels guilty. Demeter, not Zeus, is expected to nurse the children.

Fearful that she may die, Avis calls upon all her strength. Her will to live stems neither from narcissism nor from the desire for immortal fame. It rises from her sense of motherhood:

> *Her children assumed the form of awful claims upon her conscience; they presented a code to her, absolute, imperious, integral with the law of God. . . . Her will rang to the crisis. She repeated at intervals,--"It is my duty to live." (p. 331)*

79

This maiden has no mother to call her from the gate of Hades. She must play Demeter to her own Persephone. When she does propel herself from the depths to assume health and her wifely role, she sees her husband fondling the hand of a less-harried former love. Her understanding of women's traditional role is complete. She develops a deep human empathy:

> *Her great love--so hardly won, so lightly cherished--*
> *withdrew upon itself in a silence through which all the*
> *saddened lovers of the world seemed to glide with*
> *outstretched hand, and minister to her,--a mighty*
> *company. Especially her heart leaned out to all denied*
> *and deserted women, to all deceived and trustful*
> *creatures . . . . Betrayed girls, abandoned wives, aged*
> *and neglected mothers, lived in her fancy with a new,*
> *exacting claim. (p. 365)*

Later, when her son and husband die after illnesses, her sorrow is deep, but the void leaves more time for her work. She might then speak for all women through her painting. However, the years have stiffened not only her fingers but her hope, her desire, and her aspiration:

> *Avis was a careworn woman; and, like most people with*
> *whom life has dealt intensely and introspectively,*
> *the pressure of the advancing upon the retreating*
> *generation touched her personality more than her*
> *philanthropy or philosophy. Were there subtle readings*
> *of the eternal riddle astir upon the desert? Had the*
> *stone lips of the sphinx begun to mutter? God knew;*
> *and the desert knew--and the dumb mouth. (p. 451)*

Elizabeth Stuart Phelps imagistically depicts the emotions of an aspiring artist who tries to live a full, womanly life. Avis is unable to divorce herself from the expectation of others or from the frustration she feels behaving properly as wife and mother. She suffers from dual desires: to be like others (a woman, recognizable as such in her society) and to be different (an artist, removed from the necessity of seeing things in conventional, uncreative ways. Avis feels unfulfilled as woman and as artist. Phelps explicitly writes:

*We have been told that it takes three generations to
make a gentleman: we may believe that it will take as
much, or more, to make a* WOMAN. *A being of radiant
physique; the heiress of ancestral health on the maternal side; a creature forever more of nerve than of
muscle, and therefore trained to the energy of the
muscle and the repose of the nerve; physically educated
by mothers of her own fibre and by physicians of her
own sex . . . . such a creature only is competent to
the terrible task of adjusting the sacred individuality of
her life to her supreme capacity of love and the supreme
burdens and perils which it imposes upon her. (p. 450)*

Having sacrificed her career to her womanhood, Avis is left with only
the hope that her daughter, symbolically named "Wait," may do
better. Avis frequently thinks: "All was not over, the child had her life
to live. The parental resurrection came to Avis . . ." (p. 447). But
Phelps suggests that this resurrection may be nothing more than
eternal hope, for the child asks to have a story read. The novel ends
with quotations from the legend of Sir Launcelot, Sir Galahad, and the
search for the holy grail. If the female waits for the knight in shining
armor to rescue her from the drudgery of her roles, she will eternally
be receptive to the rapacious king who will force her to the world of
the dead (like Persephone) or to the cares of motherhood (like
Demeter). In any case, with or without a hero, in order to survive, she
will need to develop the strength and compassion of Demeter.


## FEAR OF FLYING

Whereas the artist speaks as mother through Avis, the artist speaks as
daughter though Isadora Wing, the heroine of Erica Jong's *Fear of
Flying* (1973). Isadora suggests that when mothers promote a non-
conventional lifestyle for their daughters, the tension between parent
and child remains electric, since the relationship is still circumscribed
by needs for love and for individuation. Her mother, for instance, says,
" 'If it weren't for you, I'd have been a famous artist,' "[49] and the
daughter thinks: "Was any of that my fault? I had spent my whole life
feeling that it was" (p. 43) Although real mothers may not say such a
cruel thing directly, their actions often telegraph this message.

81

Isadora, the heroine, believes that love is withheld from her because she has frustrated her mother's plans. She says:

> *A little gold chain chained my mother to her mother, and me to my mother. All our unhappiness was strung along the same (rapidly tarnishing) gold chain.*
>
> *Of course my mother had a rationalization for it all-- a patriarchal rationalization, the age-old rationalization of women seething with talent and ambition who keep getting knocked up.*
>
> *"Women cannot possibly do both," she said, "you've got to choose. Either be an artist or have children."*
>
> *With a name like Isadora Zelda it was clear what I was supposed to choose: everything my mother had been offered and had passed up.*
>
> *How could I possibly take off my diaphragm and get pregnant? What other women do without half thinking was for me a great and momentous act. It was a denial of my name, my destiny, my mother."* (pp. 44-45)

Conversely, by not choosing the role of mother, she is pressured by her sisters, by her in-laws, and by her husband and made to feel unwomanly. It is this expectation and her mother's martyrdom that haunt her:

> *Somewhere deep inside my head . . . is some glorious image of the ideal woman, a kind of Jewish Griselda. . . . She is a vehicle, a vessel, with no needs or desires of her own. . . . And secretly, I am always ashamed of myself for not being her.* (pp. 230-31)

This split she attributes to the image of womanhood passed along by her mother. Demeter, the mother goddess, is always both terrible and good, a fact Isadora recognizes:

> *My bad mother told me she would have been a famous artist but for me [thereby denying sustenance to her*

*hungering child], and my good mother adored me, and wouldn't have given me up for the world [thereby protecting her from the Hades of society]. What I learned from her I learned by example, not exhortation. And the lessor was clear: being a woman meant being harried, frustrated, and always angry. It meant being split into irreconcilable halves.*

*"Maybe you'll do better than me," my good mother said. "Maybe you'll do both, darling. But as for me, I never could." (p. 172)*

It is, ironically, the good mother who transmits this bad example. The artist develops a blurred self-image. The heroine's need for mothering and her need for lovers reflect Jong's needs as an artist. Her heroine recognizes the dilemma:

*If you were female and talented, life was a trap no matter which way you turned. Either you drowned in domesticity . . . or you longed for domesticity in all your art. You could never escape your femaleness. You had conflict written in your very blood. (p. 172)*

When a lover leaves her, she feels stranded in a no-person's land between two unacceptable thrones--an empty one in an underworld of her husband's and one occupied by a devouring mother. She knows that she herself is not capable of the role of self-annihilation, her view of motherhood. Phyllis Chesler has generalized about this dilemma in terms of the Demeter myth:

*Persephone does not wish to be raped, nor do women today. Neither do they wish to recapitulate their mother's identity. But the modern Persephone still has no other place to go but into marriage and motherhood. Her father (men in general) still conforms to a rape-incest model of sexuality. And her mother has not taught her to be a warrior, i.e., to take difficult roads to unknown and unique destinations--gladly. Her mother and father neither prepare her for this task nor rejoice in her success. 50*

Isadora expresses her dilemma angrily: "I was furious with my mother for not teaching me how to be a woman, for not teaching me how to make peace between the raging hunger in my cunt and the hunger in my head" (p. 168). She had to learn about women from men--writers, philosophers, psychologists--all those gods, those authorities who (she once felt) were to be trusted completely.

Early in the novel, Isadora dreams of having a girl who is different, who can break these molds. She admits, "What I really wanted was to give birth to *myself*--the little girl I might have been in a different family, a different world" (p. 51). Such a girl would not be committed, like herself and Persephone, to the underworld with father figures or to a constant rebirth in the image of her mother. At the end of the novel, she sits in a tub, tampon-string streaming in the water, sad and happy in her knowledge that she is not pregnant. "Menstruation was always a little sad--but it was also a new beginning. I was being given another chance" (p. 328). In that recognition of her body and its commitment to cycles of beginning again, she acknowledges a rebirth that she may have to experience many times over, just as Persephone does. Isadora says, "But whatever happened, I knew I would survive it. I knew, above all, that I'd go on working. Surviving meant being born over and over. It wasn't easy, and it was always painful. But there wasn't any other choice except death" (p. 339).

It is precisely this theme of constant renewal, the Demeter/Persephone myth rewritten, that runs through the fiction of the female novelist. Demeter the mother--in her desire to have her daughter by her side-- dooms Persephone to constant rebirth, constant pain, and the knowledge that death waits seasonally. The fear of this death affects both mothers and daughters as artists.

## THE GOLDEN NOTEBOOK

Anna Wulf, Doris Lessing's heroine in *The Golden Notebook* (1962), remembers very little of her own mother because she died so early; but there are times when Anna is "able to form for herself the image of somebody strong and dominating" (p. 41), whom she must fight.

If Anna plays the role of Persephone, it is in the guise of having eaten the seed of the pomegranate and being committed to the ravisher. She feels loved and loving only when a man indicates his need for all of her. Anna believes, "There is only one real female orgasm and that is when a man, from the whole of his need and desire takes a woman and wants all her response" (p. 186). Yet she herself recognizes that if this is the basis of her emotional life with men, she has no control, and is condemning herself to a desert (p. 279). Her self-image as a diseased person is caused partly by this somewhat warped view of her relationship with men and partly by her role as mother.

She calls that feeling which takes hold of her "the housewife's disease":

> *The tension in me, so that peace has already gone away from me, is because the current has been switched on: I must-dress-Janet-get-her-breakfast-send-her-off-to-school-get-Michael's-breakfast-don't-forget-I'm-out-of-tea,-etc.-etc. With this useless but apparently unavoidable tension resentment is also switched on. Resentment against what? An unfairness. That I should have to spend so much of my time worrying over details. The resentment focuses itself on Michael; although I know with my intelligence it has nothing to do with Michael. And yet I do resent him, because he will spend his day, served by secretaries, nurses, women in all kinds of capacities, who will take this weight off him.*
> (p. 285)

Only through analysis has she learned "that the resentment, the anger, is impersonal. It is the disease of women in our time" (p. 285). She cannot be angry at men, for she realizes that she, too, would be demanding and childish, the same as her lover, if she had not become a mother. She says, "The control and discipline of being a mother came so hard to me, that I can't delude myself that if I'd been a man, and not forced into self-control, I'd have been any different" (p. 286). Lessing obviously does not perceive Demeter's role as instinctual. Although she calls the discipline and resentment of caring for others "the disease of women in our time," it was obviously present one hundred years ago in Phelps' time as well. The fact is that biology commits women to a long period of nurturing their young. The role of motherhood eventually transforms both the offspring and the player of that role.

85

It is precisely this transformation that Anna wants, somehow, to postpone for her daughter, who would otherwise accept her nurturing role in accepting her sexual identity. Looking at Janet sleeping peacefully, Anna ponders their interrelationship:

> *I think that she will retain the peace for years, until the pressure comes on her, and she must start thinking. In half an hour I must remember to cook the potatoes and then I must write a list for the grocer and then I must remember to change the collar on my dress and then . . . I want very much to protect her from the pressure, to postpone it; then I tell myself I must protect her from nothing, this need is really Anna wanting to protect Anna. (p. 287)*

Lessing has identified the problem for the modern, conscious Demeter, aware of her terrible aspect.

In recalling Persephone, Demeter recalls her own carefree maidenhood. Persephone then becomes property, torn between two deities, between the motherly love of Demeter and the lustful desire of Pluto. In Ovid's version of the myth, the emphasis is on theft, robbery, and insistence on the return of property. Demeter will bear the ravishment of her daughter, but she wants her property back. Zeus is compelled to divide the year in half "so that the goddess / May be with both and either."[51] "With neither" seems to be the status of the modern artist. Torn between womanhood (as defined by society) and her need for approval, the carefree maiden/artist is constrained.

Anna not only wants but needs her daughter. To establish her identity and her *raison d'être,* Anna Wulf depends on motherhood. When she feels flat, nervous, dead, she can still, for her daughter, be calm, responsible, and alive. She plays the role and pretends, for Janet's sake, to be living. Through motherhood, a woman has some control over external order and some acceptable, approved, reason for existence.

In the course of the novel, Janet is sent to school. On the platform of the train station, seeing the young girl, her sexuality covered by the severity of her dress, Anna thinks:

> *My poor child, if you are going to grow up in a society
> full of Ivors and Ronnies, full of frightened men who
> measure out emotions like weighed groceries, then
> you'll do well to model yourself on Miss Street, the
> head-mistress. I was feeling, because that charming
> young girl had been put out of sight, as if something
> infinitely precious and vulnerable had been saved from
> hurt. And there was a triumphant malice in it, directed
> against men: All right, so you don't value us?--then
> we'll save ourselves against the time when you do
> again. (pp. 467-68)*

In Anna's world, males are expected to desire females, to want to
ravish them. Yet Anna deplores the cold, cruel rapaciousness of men
acting out their need for power in financial dealings or in an act of
unfeeling sexuality. She would no doubt rather read Pluto's rape of
Persephone as an enactment of a deep sensual commitment. In any
case, if men are becoming impotent from their fear of women, or if
their terror is manifest in homosexuality or in cold sexual acts, then this
Demeter will hide her Persephone so that she will not wander in
pastures looking for narcissus or phallic lilies.

Later, Anna realizes that by putting Janet away from men, she has also
put Janet away from herself. There is no need to rescue her, no need to
protect her. Devoid of the need to get up, Anna becomes depressed;
her life has no outer shape. She becomes aware of a new temporal
situation:

> *I haven't moved, at ease, in time, since Janet was born.
> Having a child means being conscious of the clock,
> never being free of something that has to be done at a
> certain moment ahead. An Anna is coming to life that
> died when Janet was born. (p. 468)*

Being a mother commits one to the clock and paradoxically erases time.
Just as Demeter relives her life as a maiden through Persephone, Anna
remembers an earlier self and earlier roles. Though she feels a responsibility to her daughter, she recognizes the symbiosis which may doom
them.

As Anna explains to Mother Suger (her conventional psychoanalyst who identifies ills by naming them according to myth, such as Electra, Antigone) a myth sometimes traps people into role-playing. She knows that the modern Persephone and Demeter are no longer a part of the same cultural conditions that fostered the old ones; she does not wish to be trapped in their molds.

Recognizing new conditions, Anna says, "I want to be able to separate in myself what is old and cyclic, the recurring history, the myth, from what is new, what I feel or think that might be new . . ." (p. 404).

This statement is recorded in one of five notebooks, devices Anna uses to separate areas of her life into some rational order. But life is not always rational; emotions produce absurd behavior. The several aspects of her life become chaotic; the record is fragmented. Fiction and reality intertwine. She lives a scene and then includes it in her fiction; she fictionalizes a scene and then lives it. Lessing suggests that an interrelationship between life and literature molds the image of women and entices them to fit that mold. However, without such constructs, women cannot define themselves.

Lessing holds in abeyance the mother and allows Anna the woman her madness. The author writes:

> *Yet she knew she was mad. And while she could not prevent herself from the careful obsessed business of reading masses of print, and cutting out pieces, and pinning them all over her walls, she knew that on the day Janet came home from school, she would become Anna, Anna the responsible, and the obsession would go away. She knew that Janet's mother being sane and responsible was far more important than the necessity of understanding the world; and one thing depended on the other. The world would never get itself understood, be ordered by words, be 'named,' unless Janet's mother remained a woman who was able to be responsible.* (p. 556)

The intelligent woman, driven by a need to comprehend, to order, or to explain the world does not feel whole unless she attempts to assuage this need. However, her identity as a mother makes her view relationships to others as far more important than knowledge or words. Unless one's dealings with other human beings are responsible and nurturing, an understanding of the world is impossible. Patriarchal naming will never be truthful unless it includes, with the words, a sense of the importance of interaction between human beings, a sense of nurturance.

Knowing that Janet will be home in a month, Anna, obsessed with the written word, dreams of her responsibility as a mother: "She knew it was a dream she had often had before, in one form or another. She had two children. One was Janet, plump and glossy with health. The other was Tommy, a small baby, and she was starving him. Her breasts were empty, because Janet had had all the milk in them . . ." (p. 556). Recognizing that the "starved" figure of the dream might be anyone, she experiences a vague sense of guilt. Tommy is the only one who was allowed to read her notebooks; thereafter, he attempted suicide. Her writing does not nourish; her breasts do. Compelled as a woman to nourish others, Anna feels committed to such roles. The novel ends with Anna hurrying to get back to Janet, whom she does not want to leave alone.

Anna discovers that, whatever else is new, the recurring history of motherhood is eternal. Despite her desire "to shout and scream and break everything down" (p. 566), she responds to others' needs. Having a child makes her responsible and keeps her sane (p. 556). The novel is a paradox, a novel of the artist as heroine who denies her talent as novelist and develops the art of maternal nurturance. Lessing suggests that the latter provides more sustenance to the world than "naming" does. The male writers complete their novels, unrestrained by children. The cycle has not changed much from Ovid's day. In his version of the myth, Persephone's father admits, "She is our daughter truly, yours and mine, / A common bond, a common care," [52] but the abductor, his brother, remains unpunished, and Zeus himself remains on the mountain top, dispensing gifts and judgment, removed from the pressure, details, and burden of motherhood.

# SAVE ME THE WALTZ

Mundane details seem to confine the modern Demeter and Persephone to a loss of power. When Alabama Beggs, the heroine of Zelda Fitzgerald's *Save Me the Waltz* (1932), wants her own way, her father says, "If you want to choose, you must be a goddess" (p. 204). Alabama learns through experience that it isn't easy to be a goddess away from Olympus, since the father figure defines what makes a goddess.

She, too, has an epiphany which allows her the illusion of separation from Millie, her mother: "She saw her mother as she was, part of a masculine tradition. Millie did not seem to notice about her own life, that there would be nothing left when her husband died. He was the father of her children, who were girls, and who had left her for the families of other men" (p. 201). The illusion of a severed cycle is soon shattered.

After an abortive attempt at an independent career, Alabama tries to arrange things so that her daughter will look back on *her* parents, and, as the heroine says:

> *"She will find a beautiful harmonious mosaic of two gods of the hearthstone. Looking on this vision, she will feel herself less cheated that at some period of her life she has been forced to sacrifice her lust for plunder to protect what she imagines to be the treasure that we have handed on to her. It will lead her to believe that her restlessness will pass."* (p. 206)

A tongue-twister, this passage presents a bleak image, focusing on the sacrifice rather than the joy of motherhood. This Demeter is setting the cycle in motion again, despite her realization that an awareness of woman's condition is, in effect, a betrayal of traditions. The novelist, depicting the heroine as a Persephone divided between husband and motherhood, perpetually committed to death and rebirth, structures the novel to suggest the continuity of that cycle.

## THE ODYSSEY OF KATINOU KALOKOVICH

Whereas Alabama returns to the abode of her mother with some resignation, the heroine of Natalie Petesch's *The Odyssey of Katinou Kalokovich* (1974) returns seething with the injustice of enforced role-playing. This maiden wants to break the cycle of Demeter/Persephone.

As a young girl, Katinou sees that the perpetual cycle is not easily broken. Nevertheless, she furiously resists playing out her role:

> I am a real person and I will get out of this muck. *But her sense of identification with her mother was so intense, it was like being sucked into the sea . . . Her mother had been a brave woman of unusual intelligence. . . . Yet her mother had not escaped; her marriage to Jacob K. now seemed to Kate the ultimate entrapment, and convicted Channa (in her daughter's view), of some genetic fault against which she, Kate, must be eternally vigilant: Kate saw it in herself, for instance, in the way she held her coffee cup. Just like Channa. In the way her eyes narrowed with rage. Just like Channa. In the way, when she was nervous, she plucked gingerly at a torn hangnail till it bled. The fault was there: if she were not careful, it would surely get her. (pp. 59-60)*

Despite the fact that these two women share common blood and a common destiny, Kate's disdain for the role of motherhood and the snare she perceives there separates her, positionally, from the woman she loves: "Kate stared at her mother, her heart wrung with pity. The cultural gap between them was so great that they could never make any discovery about each other when they talked . . ." (p. 109).

When her mother is weakened by the birth of a third child, the adult Katinou returns and perceives with intense feeling the kind of sacrifices women endure:

> *This then, was the way it was. Her mother had been through it for her, then for Yasha, and now for the new baby. None of these trials could have been predictable*

> *ordeals; each one in turn must have been fought over,*
> *resigned to, and finally succumbed to . . . . The burden*
> *was such that no one talked about it . . . . (p. 205)*

Kate is compelled to take full responsibility for the baby when her mother returns to a sanatorium. Petesch humorously but didactically indicates the condition of the female artist confined in the role of Demeter. Kate assumes the role of housewife and mother--sweeping, cleaning the house, dressing the baby, and finally resting beside the baby carriage on the porch, having lulled the child to sleep there. With free time available, she wants to get her sketching materials but fears leaving the baby alone. She begins to think of things that could happen to the child: ''Appalled at the monstrous possibilities dredged up by her imagination, she sat shaking with impotence'' (p. 210). Fear of the vicissitudes of life, not for herself, but for her ward, stops her temporarily from the pursuit of her own interests. She is beginning to experience the emotions of motherhood.

When she eventually does get her tools, she finds herself drawing the sacred family. Angry that she has succumbed to this tradition, she changes the painting, transforming the father and mother figures into harried creatures and devoting the most care to the transformation of the child which she had previously drawn with care and pride:

> *Kate now prepared to sacrifice the child. She must free*
> *herself from the love trap even if she had to gnaw*
> *off her own foot to do it. She transformed the baby's*
> *golden locks into hard wiry strands; she left one eye*
> *open like a wary cat's, the other winked shut with*
> *obscene coquetry. . . . Kate painted first white, then*
> *black circles around his eyes, like a clown; the slats of*
> *of the baby's high chair were rendered as bars separat-*
> *ing the three framed figures from the world. The*
> *painting which had been one of any family in the world*
> *had become transmogrified into a Daumier-portrait of*
> *the Damned. She called it* The Trap. *(pp. 215-16)*

Instead of glorifying motherhood, she wants people to see the drawbacks and be frightened by the burdens. Despite this aggressive action, she wants to cry. She feels free to be neither womanly, according to society's definitions, nor creative, according to her own. She is lured from her self-pity by the need to prepare dinner and otherwise drudge in work that will detract from rather than nourish her artistic imagination. Petesch suggests that even if women elect to be childless, they are trapped into "mothering," into affiliation with others, into accepting the burdens of nurturance. Persephone is forced into the role of Demeter, even though she may prefer to roam in the open fields. The dual desires--to be as free as Persephone before the rape and as womanly as Demeter--pull the female artist in each direction. Frequently, as in Petesch's novel, the tension develops from a rejection of the mother-as-example.

## LADY ORACLE

Margaret Atwood, in two novels focusing on mother/daughter/artist relationships, registers this fear of her heroines. In *Lady Oracle* (1976), the narrator frets: "I wanted children, but what if I had a child who would turn out like me? Even worse, what if I turned out to be like my mother? All this time I carried my mother around my neck like a rotting albatross." [53] The stench of this association pervades Joan Foster's life.

Joan's mother provides a negative example of behavior for her daughter, partly because Mrs. Foster depends on the approval of others. The time she spends before mirrors, putting on cosmetics, manifests that dependency and her need for masking. Joan dreams about the act in mythic images:

> *Although her vanity tables became more grandiose as my father got richer, my mother always had a triple mirror, so she could see both sides as well as the front of her head. In the dream, as I watched, I suddenly realized that instead of three reflections she had three actual heads, which rose from her toweled shoulders on three separate necks. (pp. 66-67)*

As a young girl, she wants to keep her mother's monstrous nature a secret from any man who would enter her mother's bedroom (presumably, from her father). As she grows older, she wants this "mysterious man" to find out that her mother is "a monster" (p. 67).

Searching for causes, Joan decides that her mother's grotesqueness stems partly from her lack of purpose. The heroine explains:

> It wasn't that she was aggressive and ambitious, although she was both these things. Perhaps she wasn't aggressive or ambitious enough. If she'd ever decided what she really wanted to do and had gone out and done it, she wouldn't have seen me as a reproach to her, the embodiment of her own failure and depression, a huge edgeless cloud of inchoate matter which refused to be shaped into anything for which she could get a prize. (p. 67)

In this passage explicating the cause of Mrs. Foster's hideous nature, the heroine implies her mother's need for approval and her own monstrosity as the embodiment of her mother's failure. A conversation she overheard as a child helped to create this self-image. She knows that, as an unwanted baby, she prompted her parents' marriage. Her mother wanted an abortion, but her father, though a medical man, would not make the arrangements.

Aware of her mother's intended rejection, Joan continually longs for her mother's approval. She buys a three-sided mirror like her mother's and attempts automatic writing while sitting before the candle-lit mirrors. The attempt to fuse artist and mother figure is quite evident in this act. Demeter and Persephone reverse roles. Joan's dead mother calls to her from the shadows of the mirror. The attraction continues throughout the heroine's life.

Although she does not want to identify positionally with Mrs. Foster and spend her life "in a cage, as a fat whore, a captive Earth Mother" (p. 328), she is drawn personally by the need of her mother's approval. Joan sleepwalks toward the vision of her mother on the balcony: "I loved her but the glass was between us, I would have to go through it. I longed to console her. Together we would go down the corridor into the darkness. I would do what she wanted" (p. 329). She describes a joint descent to the underworld as she nearly plummets to her death.

94

Awakened by the cold air after crashing through the window, Joan realizes:

> She'd come very close that time, she'd almost done it. She's never really let go of me because I had never let her go. It had been she standing behind me in the mirror, she was the one who was waiting around each turn, her voice whispered the words. She had been the lady in the boat, the death barge, the tragic lady with flowing hair and stricken eyes, the lady in the tower. She couldn't stand the view from the window, life was her curse. How could I renounce her? She needed her freedom also; she had been my reflection too long. (pp. 329-30)

Joan renounces her mother's position, her entrapment, and her behavior but cannot renounce the love she has for Mrs. Foster. The torment of their relationship "fosters" Joan's poetry and her fiction. The heroine admits, "My mother was a vortex, a dark vacuum, I would never be able to make her happy. Or anyone else. Maybe it was time for me to stop trying" (p. 330). But the process of separation is difficult.

Her final commitment in this novel is to the real romance of her life--the desire to play Houdini, the escape artist who, entering the embrace of bondage, can slither out again from the womb of the locked and submerged trunk. She can only dream of such an escape; like Houdini, she is mortal.

## SURFACING

The heroine of Atwood's *Surfacing* (1972) is also bound by a mortal existence, despite her entry into a mythic realm. The heroine originally claims, "Impossible to be like my mother, it would need a time warp . . . ." [54] Yet the mother becomes her guiding spirit into a world of specters and a new *mythos*.

The narrator searches the Canadian woods for her father, not realizing that he has joined her mother in the world of the dead. Looking through pictures for clues of her father, the narrator is disturbed by her own past. She had followed the advice of a self-seeking man in a mechanized society and aborted their child. Trying to insure her parent's innocence, she had kept the abortion a secret. In her present search through clues, she feels that her parents may offer a connection to a reality she desperately needs. She wins from her father, after his death, the talisman of oracular, mythic Indian drawings which he had discovered. Searching for her mother's gift, she explains:

> More than ever I needed to find it, the thing she had hidden; the power from my father's intercession wasn't enough to protect me, it gave only knowledge and there were more gods than his, his were the gods of the head, antlers rooted in the brain. (p. 153)

Eventually she finds what she believes is her mother's legacy, a crayon drawing:

> The gift itself was a loose page, the edge torn, the figures drawn in crayon. On the left was a woman with a round moon stomach: the baby was sitting up inside her gazing out. Opposite her was a man with horns on his head like cow horns and a barbed tail.
>
> The picture was mine. (p. 158)

As a child, she was not aware of its symbolism. As a young woman, she relates to the mythic power of motherhood, a physical power quite different from the intellectual and demonic power of her father. Taking her lover outside in the woods, she enacts the rites of transformation. She believes herself to be pregnant, based on biological timing. When the others want to leave the cabin for civilization, she slips into a canoe, abandons them and their life, and becomes part of the land and the water. Relating to her mother's spirit in the garden upon returning to the cabin alone, she strips herself of all forms of civilization and grovels in the dirt, losing contact with a machine age of murderers and turning herself into a "new kind of centrefold"--the natural, dirty woman (p. 190). Rising from earth and lake, this unnamed heroine bears within her an embryo, an amphibian creature.

Even with the awe-inspiring quality of motherhood to give her giant proportions in the wilderness, this heroine must accept the human condition. To form a healthy baby, she needs outside help. A male ambassador from civilization (perhaps a budding Triptolemus) calls her forth. Remaining hidden, she is tempted to respond. Although this ending may consequently be read in many ways, the essential point is the necessity for new beginnings.

Atwood suggests the need for renewal by way of the natural world, an understanding of the past, spiritual connections between women and their mothers, and the use of head and body to evaluate actions. Through mythic images with a primordial quality, Atwood moves the reader to return with her heroine to appreciate life-giving sources, to mourn the loss of natural surroundings, and to deplore the wanton killing of fish, birds, and babies. She glorifies the maternal qualities which would protect life on all levels. In advocating wholeness, she stresses the biological knowledge of motherhood to counterbalance the inordinate attention which has been given the intellectual knowledge of the father.

However, in evoking, worshipping, and identifying with her mother's spirit, the heroine assumes not only the motherly role but its mythic proportions, which overshadow any individual identity she might have as a woman in other realms. As an initiate to the mysteries, she cannot remain an impartial observer. In embracing her mother and the condition of motherhood, the heroine willingly sacrifices her art. Life-giving sources of the mother take precedence over the life-stilling powers of the father. In rewriting the myth of Demeter and Persephone to suggest the dignity of maiden and mother in a natural rather than a mechanized, sterile, or institutionalized estate, Atwood sacrifices both the artist and the *Künstlerroman* to this new *mythos,* which is a return to the underworld and another beginning. In so powerful a presentation, Atwood suggests the pull which the mother/daughter relationship must have on her as an artist.

## MRS. STEVENS HEARS THE MERMAIDS SINGING

In a more obvious acknowledgment of mother as muse, May Sarton wrote *Mrs. Stevens Hears the Mermaids Singing* (1965). Whereas

Atwood's heroine removes herself from the super-conscious world of the Faustian meditator, May Sarton's heroine tries intellectually to comprehend the source of art in general, the peculiar differences between the art of males and of females, and the nature of her art source in particular.

One of the most obvious difficulties of a woman artist seems to Mrs. Stevens to be the time she spends on mundane details. She thinks, "It was all very well to insist that art had no sex, but the fact was that the days of men were not in the same way fragmented, atomized by indefinite small tasks."[55] Whether true or not, her thoughts concerning these details are relevant. Although Hilary Stevens is not a mother, she "mothers" people, cares for the atmosphere which she provides for them, and frets over their well-being. A long passage is indicative of her thoughts:

> "They" always said, "What beautiful flowers you have!" But "they" never imagined how much time this irrelevant passion took from her work, at least an hour every morning in summer. No man would trouble about such things; the imaginary man in her mind got up at six, never made his bed, did not care a hoot if there were a flower or not, and was at his desk as bright as a button, at dawn, with a whole clear day before him while some woman out of sight was making a delicious hot stew for his supper. Hilary had often asked herself why she felt the need for flowers . . . , but there it was. The house felt empty and desolate without them. They were silent guests who must be made happy, and who gave the atmosphere a kind of soul. She went out with her scissors and cut two or three daffodils . . . and a few poeticus narcissi . . . . (p. 36)

The passage suggests a conflict common to women: a pride in their ability to provide a comfortable and lovely atmosphere and a shame in the "irrelevance" of such an undertaking. The conflict provokes them to imagine that men's lives are free of interruptions.

The irritation or jealousy with which Sarton arms Hilary Stevens is similar to that Anna Wulf experiences. Both are jealous of a supposed freedom from housekeeping duties. The fact that men have their own form of interruptions which may be just as irritating to them is not so important as the fact that Anna Wulf and Hilary Stevens (perhaps women in general) *imagine* them to be relatively free from irrelevant activity. Despite the fact that Mrs. Stevens has an acquaintance who works for her in the garden and a housekeeper whom she could direct to cut and arrange flowers, she feels duty-bound to care personally for details in the home. She goes so far as to "mother" the flowers: "They were silent guests who must be made happy" (p. 36). Even Hilary Stevens wonders why.

When married, she felt restricted by what she considered to be a trivial life and caged even more by the demands of housekeeping: "House-keeping terrified and absorbed her, and she felt challenged to a kind of perfectionism which gave her no leeway as far as time went" (p. 43). A successful novelist at that time, she nevertheless felt bound to let the housekeeping chores "absorb" her time and energy. The obligation and the challenge come from a yearning for approval as a woman and a need to identify with the mother figure. In order to do so, she feels she must relinquish her selfish needs as an artist. Hilary confides to her understanding mother-in-law: " 'It is hard to be a woman and a writer. Lately, I have begun to think it impossible. I want to feel sane and whole' " (p. 47). Though completely sensitive to her daughter-in-law's needs as an artist, the elder Mrs. Stevens can only sympathize: " 'I settled for being a woman. I wonder whether you can' " (p. 47). Both women assume that being a woman and being an artist are not compatible goals, primarily because they define womanliness in terms of giving of themselves, of mothering. The elder Mrs. Stevens recognizes Hilary's touch of genius but she also warns her, " 'Life with Adrian is going to ask all your tenderness, all your womanliness . . .' " (p. 47).

The dilemma of choosing is eliminated by her husband's early death, but the conflict between her sense of womanhood and her artistry is not resolved. The source of the conflict is the memory of her mother. As a child, Hilary had once shouted, " 'I'm nothing like you or Pa and being like you would kill me!' " (p. 62). Admitting that she had always felt her father's love as a certainty, she finds her mother's feelings more complicated and less obvious:

*Tenderness was only safe if given or received by the*
*sick in bed and no wonder Hilary spent such large*
*numbers of weeks as a child being ill! No wonder she*
*had reacted so violently all her life to the fear of feeling,*
*and to the fury who attended it, the sense of guilt.*
*(p. 62)*

Hilary obviously needs her mother's approval, desires physical
intimacy, and must establish a sexual identity which she is trained to
abhor. While growing up, she learned to consider all bodily functions as
being indelicate. Her relationship to her own body is therefore tinged
with guilt.

Tense before an interview in her own home, she wishes that her mother
could have been proud. Hilary admits that she wanted recognition from
her mother and never got it. Though other people may praise Hilary for
her art, she feels the need to excel in domestic activities, as well, so
that she can identify with if not receive approval from her mother.
Trained to believe that the important things in life are people and
personal relationships (p. 150), Hilary Stevens and the female inter-
viewer--a poet and reporter--both agree that women who choose to be
something more and something less than women are somehow
monsters. Both believe that a woman, biologically engineered to create
children instead of works of art, is meant to mother. Therefore, a
woman who constructs objects outside of herself and her family is
abnormal. But, Mrs. Stevens says, "For the aberrant woman, art is
health, the only health," for without this release she would go mad.
Mrs. Stevens explains:

*"The woman who needs to create works of art is born*
*with a kind of psychic tension in her which drives her*
*unmercifully to find a way to balance, to make herself*
*whole. Every human being has this need: in the artist it*
*is mandatory. Unable to fulfill it, he goes mad. But*
*when the artist is a woman she fulfills it at the* expense
*of herself as a woman." (p. 191)*

Ironically, the need to find release from psychic tension through art is
counterbalanced by the need for approval as a woman.

One way out of the dilemma is to identify with a strong female. In talking to the reporters about the identity of the muses for each group of poems she created, Mrs. Stevens reveals that each muse was a loved one, a strong model or a powerful antagonist, usually a woman, who fostered emotions which were molded into poetry. The loved one is "the person of the epiphany" (p. 125). But Mrs. Stevens, in commenting that her mother "still remains the great devouring enigma" (p. 193), understands in another epiphanic moment that she was the ultimate muse. Mrs. Stevens explains: " 'When my mother died I experienced desolation, and at the same time . . . a freedom which had suddenly become pointless. . . . She was in a queer way *the* antagonist, you see, the one who still had to be persuaded' " (p. 193). A woman's difficulty in the process of individuation is exemplified by Mrs. Stevens' feelings of both release and sorrow at the death of her mother. Mother and daughter must be separated in order to establish individual identities, but the process is painful for them. For the artist, it is doubly difficult. Her understanding of womanhood usually includes the notion of caring for and uniting with others. That understanding can retard the establishment not only of her own identity but of her art as well. Hilary Stevens tries to explain what she believes the woman artist strives for:

> *"Never to categorize, never to separate one thing from*
> *another--intellect, the senses, the imagination, . . .*
> *some total gathering together where the most realistic*
> *and the most mystical can be joined in a celebration*
> *of life itself. Women's work is always toward whole-*
> *ness." (p. 172)*

Agreeing with Hilary that this explanation "does sound vague" (p. 172), I believe its importance lies in the fact that it suggests the need to obliterate the self. Certainly all artists, both male and female, strain toward wholeness, toward a unified vision. However, Dorothy Richardson's jumble of details suggesting the existence of only one level of reality; Atwood's connection of her heroine and mythical spirits; Virginia Woolf's meshing of sea, art, and life and her warping of time boundaries; Lessing's multiple notebooks; and May Sinclair's mystical suspension of will are all unique urges toward wholeness which have their counterparts in the expression of men. But the artist/ heroine's sense of wanting to become one with her mother, to identify with her as a woman, and the conflicting need to separate from her as an individual and as an artist seem to be the sole province of the female. To each female artist, as to Mrs. Stevens, the mother is "the Muse" who "destroys as well as gives life, does not nourish, pierces, forces one to discard, renew, be born again. Joy and agony are pivoted in her presence" (p. 186).

In *Mrs. Stevens Hears the Mermaids Singing*, the male interviewer believes he has identified the unique quality of female art. He says, "The feminine genius is the genius of self-creation" (p. 196). But every artist must create a self, an identity which refashions either the self or the restrictions of the world. If there is a distinctly "feminine" art form, at least in the novel of the artist as heroine, it is the underlying tension which stems from two needs : the need for total wholeness and the need to create a separate self, both of which are connected to the daughter/mother relationship. The "mothering" artist longs for the relative independence of her maidenhood; the independent artist needs approval from, the love of, and an identification with the mother. The Demeter/Persephone cycle seems to continue even in the modern *Künstlerroman*.

## HER MOTHERS

One contemporary novel that both repeats and rewrites the myth is E.M. Broner's *Her Mothers* (1975), which begins with a modern-day Demeter searching for her Persephone. The husband/father is absent. In this novel Demeter, in the guise of Beatrix Palmer, searches not only for her daughter, but for her own "mothers" and for herself. The dialogues between mother and daughter form a ritual tracing women's history, real or imagined. For instance, an unidentified daughter says, " 'Mother, I'm giving birth to a poetess.' " The abstract and unidentified mother responds with the irony of the ages, saying, " 'Tell her there's no such thing.' " 56

The narrator plays the role of dragon-slayer or ritual-slaughterer. Both roles have double meanings. Traditionally, dragons are females. The knight in shining armor "slays" the dragon or magically subdues her power. As a female performing this role, the heroine is both the dragon-lady and the dragon-slayer. By assuming the power of execution, she runs the risk of killing the female within. In another twist, the

102

ritual-slaughterer may be interpreted two ways. Traditionally a man who slays the sacrificial animal, the ritual-slaughterer may also be considered a person who does away with traditional rituals. The female ritual-slaughterer is an anachronism--a part of a ritual which doesn't include her, an executioner of such rituals, and, consequently, a creator of new traditions. Though fearful and trembling in this role, she is also awesome, especially to her daughter.

Whereas the narrator presents Beatrix's viewpoint, the daughter's feelings are recorded in a notebook. One particular passage reflects the anxieties of her generation:

> "Now Mrs. Kennedy is pregnant with an eleventh child and there are the constant assassinations, assassinations as common as births. I cry & mother weeps, tears falling on my head in her lap. I don't understand and therefore no words, no logical, comprehending words come to calm me. I am 16 & it is unfair that people at 16 must think about the country's fate, must experience the pain.

> "Come, Hades, give me a taste of your medicine. Cure me of the life force. Last week at Jim's I tried your medicine, powerful Hades. And mother found me and laughed and screamed, 'You are sick. If I had the money I'd put you in an institution,' and I, in my pain, hear her laughing scream, and she slaps me to show me how much she loves me, and the doctor on the radio tells of slapping Kennedy to hear a heartbeat and the pulse, and he hands the stethoscope to Ethel Kennedy to listen." (pp. 230-31)

Constructed or programmed to be sensitive to the needs of others, women experience pain in human relations, pain such as that highlighted in this passage. Through their own bodies, women are introduced to balances and imbalances connected with love, pain, death, and birth. They know of blood and of rebirth through blood. Other lessons, like submission, unappeased longing, psychological crippling (sometimes from rape, sometimes from fear of rape), the burden of womanhood--these messages are telegraphed from mother to daughter. The two cling to one another, devour one another, reject one another, and long yet again for one another. The heroines of *Her Mothers* are no exception; Lena and Beatrix suffer through these separations and reunions.

One of the reunions of this novel's Demeter and Persephone is described after the fact of a violent scene: "The mother will be left, bereft. They had drowned each other first in tears and then had almost drowned each other" (p. 239). Staring at the road past the most recent departure of her daughter, Beatrix ponders:

> *Had she wheeled the yellow-lined carriage into the Gulf? Was she strangling that baby with her red scarf when she nurtured her? Was she pressing that face into her chest to keep the nose from breathing?*
> (p. 240)

The modern Demeter has increased worries. She feels not only joy and sorrow but guilt, for omissions and commissions. As Adrienne Rich explains, "Mothering and nonmothering have been such charged concepts for us, precisely because *whichever we did has been turned against us.* "[57] In an age of increasing consciousness, institutions filled with psychologists, professors, advertisers, and criminal lawyers demand much from the mother. They remind her of her power to influence for good and bad. Under such pressure, she often feels impotent. If she protects Persephone, she may be guilty of overprotection. If she is not protective, she may lose the daughter's love as well as her companionship.

In *Her Mothers,* the ritual slaughterer tries to break the dispiriting chains of the institution of motherhood. Envisioning a future generation of independent mothers and daughters, E.M. Broner creates a Persephone who returns of her own free will. Walking toward her mother, Lena says, " 'No more assassinations' " (p. 241). The three words carry many messages: They plead for the end of a patriarchal society which creates assassins. They plead for a release from "mothering" that devours instead of nourishes. They recognize "the final generosity" (p. 116), which is to embrace one's mother rather than wait for her embrace. They remind the world to honor mothers of previous generations, who "were not trained to run the race, and, when a few of them did, their chests ached, their legs stiffened, they panted long before the finish line" (p. 126). They remind women, in the voice of the narrator, to "choose carefully, for we can pick and choose not only our mothers but among their qualities!" (p. 79). Most of all, they beg women to stop assassinating themselves and one another.

By exhorting women to venerate all mothers of strength, including historical mothers who have nurtured for centuries, E.M. Broner resurrects the healing and energizing powers which accompanied the Eleusinian mysteries. The glorification of Demeter begins again, not in the worship of passive, biological motherhood, but in admiration for any mother's courage, persistence, intelligence, and active compassion. In this new *mythos,* Demeter still insists on the return of her daughter from the power of a patriarchal realm. She still nourishes in joy and in sorrow. But, by struggling to re-define herself, the modern Demeter demonstrates new possibilities for her daughters.[58] Despite her heroine's limited success in communicating as a mother with her daughter, despite her failure even as a writer to provide words of comfort to her daughter, Beatrix offers the legacy of a battling spirit. From it, Lena learns to resist destructive forces, to fight tyranny, and even to escape her "devouring" mother. More important, Lena becomes strong enough to return on her own, to "mother" her own mother, to embrace her as an independent being, as a daughter and a mother. In demanding her own independence, the modern Demeter can release the daughters within and without.

However, the novel neither advocates nor accomplishes a break in the mother/daughter cycle. Instead, it emphasizes the positive aspect of this cycle through the artist/mother. She may doubt her effectiveness as a mother; she may chafe under the restrictions that motherhood brings to her art. But her strong and continued fight to do both affords Lena a choice of lifestyles. In the end, the narrator intones her own plea:

> *Birth me, Mothers. Carry me in the brine of your belly*
> *and your tears.*
>
> *Let us sit on each others' laps, daughters and mothers.*
> (*p. 241*)

105

The cathexis of emotions which surround the mother/daughter relationship generates this novel of the artist as heroine. A release from the fear of expressing those emotions provides the epiphany at the end, an acknowledgment of the boon such a relationship offers.

The plea summarizes the generating force of most *Künstlerromanen* written by and about women. It calls for support and approval from the mother, indicates a split in the speaker's needs to identify with the mother and to play the role of the relatively independent daughter, requests a rebirth, suggests the sorrow concomitant with the female condition, stresses the biological processes which form and control women, asks for and offers nurturance, and joins rather than individuates mothers and daughters. Directed to "Mothers," the plea suggests the eternal or widespread nature of the cycle. The recognition of that cycle mirrors the *anagnorisis* present in the Eleusinian mysteries venerating Demeter/Persephone. The new *mythos* incorporates the old.

## Chapter IV

# THE ARTIST AS HEROINE: HER JOURNEY TO THE INTERIOR

*"Without self-confidence we are as babes in the cradle."*[1]
*--Virginia Woolf*

*"There's more space within than without ......."*[2]
*--Dorothy Richardson*

*"I had to learn where the roots were:
and they were in me."*[3]

*--Anaïs Nin*

## BACKGROUND

Looking at myths frequently used in literature to represent the artist--
Daedalus, Icarus, Prometheus, and Faust--a woman can recognize the
roles assigned to her in real life. Traditionally, she operates as mother--
bringing into the world a divine son or an artist; as helpmate--obtaining
the thread for the labyrinth; as beauteous Aphrodite or muse--inspiring
the male artist to great heights or luring him to his downfall; or as
troublemaker--the sphinx who poses riddles, the dragon who guards
the treasure, the siren who lures men, or the Medusa who turns them to
stone. Operating within a literary tradition dependent on such myths,
the female novelist suffers disintegration. To be a heroine, she must
nurture, help, inspire; by defending her independence as an artist, she
turns into a gorgon. Consequently, if the female novelist is to depict the
heroine as a positive and active figure, she must either rewrite the old

myths or create a new *mythos*. Instead of mating with bulls, she must escape or subdue them. If imprisoned in the labyrinth by outside forces, she must fly skyward. If her heritage is menial, she must create herself in a new image. If she suffocates in traditional settings, she must find breathing space elsewhere. Attempting any of these, she risks alienating herself not only from others but from her own sexual identity.

Rebelling against tradition and family, the hero asserts his manhood in the eyes of society; fighting dragon-mothers and armored lovers, the heroine assails her womanhood as society defines it. As so determined, then, her sexual identity becomes her real enemy. Mabel Blake Cohen explains the divisiveness:

> *There is a considerable incompatibility between many people's sense of identity as persons and as sexual beings, or, to put it another way, between society's traditional definition of the person's sexual role and the optimal development of his assets as a person.* 4

This incompatibility, if it is intense, has repercussions. As Weinstein and Platt have warned: "A significant discrepancy between what one actually is or must become or do, and the ideal representation of self, if it is not corrected, leads to feelings of self-hatred, unworthiness, and the like." 5

Descending to the interior labyrinth, the artist discovers there the hatred she has for herself or for society. Unlike the hero, the heroine does not identify with demonic destructiveness and hate. For the creative artist, these urges seem contrary to her role as woman. Seeing her own monstrous or potentially destructive nature, she sometimes aborts the creative self. On the other hand, when she successfully gives birth to a creative personality, she discovers the sorrows and responsibilities she has assumed with her new offspring, which is considered inhuman.

Rollo May offers a way out of this dilemma: "Identify with that which haunts you, not in order to fight it off, but to take it into your self; for it must represent some rejected element in you." 6 But this psychotherapist also unwittingly indicates how difficult it is for a woman when he explains his belief: "The female is so often seen as daimonic because every individual, male or female, begins life with a tie to the mother." [7] He confirms the female artist's fears: The mythic demon is the Terrible Devouring Mother, the horror she must flee in order to individuate, in order to establish herself as a separate person. Neumann has defined and set the trap which awaits her. He writes, "While the specific achievement of the male world lies in the development of the masculine consciousness and the rational mind, the female psyche is in far greater degree dependent on the productivity of the unconscious." [8] To be conscious, to name, to identify, to be intelligent, to create art, is to be masculine. To be the muse of or the image in art is to be feminine. The circle is endless; it confines the female to specific roles.

When the artist must reject the mythic woman of literature written by men, must reject a stereotype of the "animus" conceptualized by Jung and used by Neumann, must ignore the theory of penis envy postulated by Freud, must fight an identification with her mother in order to individuate, and must identify with her mother in order to create the artist/woman she is, the task seems Herculean rather than feminine. She must die as this mythic "feminine" woman in order to give birth to herself as an artist, a creator of myths. For her, the journey to the interior is often an acceptance of darkness there or in the place to which she returns.

When the *Künstlerroman* focuses on the development of the artist rather than on a static moment of revelation, the novel usually takes the form of a voyage from early and innocent childhood experiences, an initiation into an underworld which threatens to blight her talent or alienate her from society, a subsequent re-evaluation of self or society, and, finally, a statement of her position in the world of people or of art. Campbell's description of the monomythic pattern, "a separation from the world, a penetration to some source of power, and a life-enhancing return," [9] need be changed only somewhat for the female version. In the voyage to subterranean or subaqueous territory, the heroine often emerges water-logged or weakened to the point of despair. Whereas the hero might be expected to emerge victorious in a battle with demons, the heroine frequently accepts her role as one of them. An examination of the journeys to the interior of several heroines in the novel of the artist will confirm this statement.

# THE STORY OF AVIS

In *The Story of Avis* (1897), Elizabeth Stuart Phelps [Ward] depicts a heroine who manages to create only one praiseworthy painting, a muted sphinx that symbolizes the paralysis she feels in trying to be both artist and woman.

In an artistic vision Avis, pondering the mystery of womanhood, hears the sphinx whisper, " 'Speak for me' " (p. 150). To become a complete woman with sexual identity firmly established, Avis chooses wifehood, motherhood, and homemaking. Living in this manner (considered womanly by society) and thus experiencing the mystery of womanhood, the artist is struck dumb--by the care of others.

Avis dives into this marriage knowing, intellectually, that her work may suffer, despite all her lover's vows to cherish her talent. Once submerged in the marriage, she experiences the sacrifice of her work as a vision, an *anagnorisis:*

> *Sitting burdened with the child upon her arms, she looked out and off upon the summer sky with a strangling desolation like that of the forgotten diver, who sees the clouds flit, from the bottom of the sea.* (p. 284)

This descent does not refresh her. Long submerged, she survives, but barely. The burdens she assumes in nurturing others drag on her spirit and her body. Understanding the problems of careworn women, she cannot act as spokeswoman for them; silenced by depression and maternal duties, she visits her studio:

> *And there she was sitting, pinioned, with both children, patient and worn, with the bright colors of paints around her, and the pictures, with their mute faces to the wall, about the room . . . .* (p. 370)

Having gone through initiation, downfall, and drowning in cares to the point of near-death, she emerges wearied and mute. When her husband, reunited with her after his infidelity, tells her that he hadn't meant to blight her future, "She felt choked, as if with a physical congestion. A passion is a passion, be it of the intellect or of the heart;

110

and a denied aspiration dies, perhaps, more dumbly, but never less drearily, than a denied love" (p. 405).

Like the dumb but wise sphinx, Avis is knowledgeable but mute. For a female who aspires, who tries to climb too high, or who actually breathes heady air in the realm of fame, the punishment is suffocation or self-alienation, either as an artist or as a woman. Having suffered, Avis journeys to the past for a reason. Puzzled by her friend's seeming contentment in the traditional roles of women, Avis is not satisfied by Coy's explanation for her tranquillity, that explanation being: " 'It is nature!' " Avis responds, " '*I* am nature, too. Explain me, Coy' " (p. 455). Many women do find fulfillment in traditional roles. The artist may be an aberration or a hybrid. Regardless, she also needs air space in the natural order of things. Without it, her sprouts will be severely dwarfed or will remain ungerminated.


## A WOMAN OF GENIUS

Mary Austin's voyage in *A Woman of Genius* (1912) takes a different route. Austin states her purpose clearly in the opening chapter. She explains that genius is an uncontrollable force operating in any individual. Society is at fault for any sordid events in the war between a woman and her genius. The *Künstlerroman* becomes a case for the defense of behavior she perceives during her introspective, retrospective journey. The novel is the battle between an artist and the society that refuses to consider her as feminine just because she is driven by an internal demon.

In her search for the cause of her dilemma, Austin's heroine is befuddled, philosophically. She states, "I was by the shock of too early maternity driven apart from the usual, and I still believe the happier, destiny of women" (p. 130). The narrator cannot have it both ways. Either her genius drives her, or her failure as the mother of a child who later dies causes her to choose a non-traditional role.

In addition to blaming her compulsive genius and her abortive experience as mother, she condemns society for her difficulties. She derides a local social leader, Pauline Mills, for never having an idea "which was not conditioned by the pattern she had set for her-

111

self . . ." (p. 266). Olivia has also set a pattern for herself but blames Pauline for rigid goals because she refuses to help Olivia financially. Forced to draw on her resources, much like trying to draw water from an empty well, Olivia complains: "I suffered many humiliations before I learned how absolutely, by that same society that so liberally resents the implication of any separateness in art, the artist is thrust back upon himself" (p. 263).

This self that desires distinctiveness, separation, individuation, also longs to be accepted, nurtured, and approved by society. If she prostitutes herself either literally or by following the demands of fashionable society and leaving the stage, she can prosper. Olivia feels buffeted by her "genius" for acting, by society's haughty insistence on its set standards, by the lack of any uncontaminated financial support, and by her own desperate need for love and approval. Using sub-aqueous images to describe her condition, she flees from all these realities, "to be ricocheted by them again on to that reef of moral squalor upon which the artist and woman in me were driven asunder" (p. 309). Although Olivia survives the buffeting, her capacity to love is "retarded, crippled" (p. 115), and her gift for acting is "cramped and enfeebled in expression, rendered tormenting in its passage and futile to the recipient . . ." (p. 59).

Austin depicts her heroine's voyage as a rough one, and her *Künstler-roman* is a bitterly-worded complaint to the shipping lines. Olivia's introspection reveals that if she is monstrous, society and outside forces have made her so. The narrator's only fear in relating "incidents difficult and sordid" is that the reading public "might still miss the point of . . . being largely to blame for them" (p. 7). Because Olivia faults circumstances and the world at large, she will not effect inward personal growth. She can only toughen the outer shell and isolate herself on the stage, playing roles for their approval. The irony is evident to the reader, if not to the writer.

## PILGRIMAGE

Compared to Austin's *Künstlerroman*, Dorothy Richardson's journey to the interior in *Pilgrimage* (1913-1957) is longer (thirteen chapter-volumes), more circuitous, and more introspective. The opening paragraph depicts the heroine, Miriam Henderson, mounting steps and describing polarities of dark and light, human relationships and solitude, silence and speech, movement and the stillness necessary for reflection on the action of a journey. These polarities persist in her motion toward the future as well as in her introspective journey to the past. To Miriam, both past and future exist in the present moment. Wanting to enjoy the miracle of that moment, she also wants to reflect and to record that enjoyment. The pull between art and life is common to any writer, but Miriam's ambivalence also stems from difficulty in the process of her individuation.

Because she is uncomfortable in roles normally assigned to women, she considers herself a man. Consequently, when she examines her life, she tries to connect with other women at the same time she wants to feel unique. Her journey to the interior takes her back to the moment she first remembers, a moment when she is free from the tug of opposing poles, a moment when she is aware only of a totality, a lack of divisiveness, and a "blazing alley of flowers without beginning or end" (II, 213). She longs for that experience of totality to return.

In trying to gain a perspective on herself and her need for solitude, she ponders, too, her need for "floods of sunshine and beauty indoors and out" (III, 243): "Was this bright shape, that drew her, the secret of her nature . . . the clue she had carried in her hand through the maze?" (III, 244). She rejects the sunshine at Newlands because women are caged in such an environment of wealth and possessions. Searching again for an acceptable model of behavior or style of life, she feels alienated. However, when a foreign-born beau satirizes English society, she is offended. She feels a kinship with English gaiety:

> *Far away in the distance, coming always nearer, was the summer morning of her infancy, a permanent standing arrested, level with the brilliance of flower-heads motionless in the sunlit air; no movement but the hovering of bees. Beyond this memory towards which she passed every day more surely, a marvellous scene unfolded. And always with the unfolding of its wide prospects, there came a beautifying breath. (III, 197)*

Looking backward and forward to a happier time of sunshine, flowers, and freedom from care, she begins to grow in the light of Michael Shatov's personal approval. The smile she wears reflects the "wise, so irritating smile" of women around her. She can identify with their vision of love and of sunshine and vistas that opened to freedom:

> *She recognized them for lonely wanderers upon the earth. They, these women, then were the only people who* knew. *Their smile was the smile of these wide vistas, wrought and shaped, held back by the pity they turned towards the blind life of men; but it was* alone *in its vision of the spaces opening beyond the world of daily life.* (III, 198)

Miriam realizes that men work with brawn or brains to build gardens; women inhabit and appreciate them. Women see the beauty of the moment, of flowers, of "being" as opposed to the rush of "becoming." The appreciation cannot be shared by men who argue their own viewpoints, who are busy making the money to buy such gardens, or who revere women provided they remain alone in the garden.

Just as she begins to identify with some women, Shatov, who wants to marry her, confesses to illicit heterosexual activities in his student days. Appalled, she sees leering European men and compares them ill-favorably with prostitutes. But to identify with women is to identify with "the whole masculine sense of womanhood. One image; perceived only with the body, separated and apart from everything else in life" (III, 208). The only other image offered is that of an idol "within a spiral of unconsuming radiance," but "the cost and demand" (III, 212) of being dependent on Shatov's worship are too much. She pulls back, independent, feeling masculine in her need for freedom and self-direction. She cannot find a way out of the maze. She says, "I'm as much a man as a woman. That's why I can't help seeing things" (III, 221).

In her need to be released from the tension of gender identity, she continually searches her past. She relives a moment,

> *exactly the same as the first one she could remember, the moment of standing, alone, in the bright sunlight on*

114

> *a narrow gravel path in the garden at Babington*
> *between two banks of flowers, the flowers level with her*
> *face, and large bees swinging slowly to and fro before*
> *her face from bank to bank ........ It was the same*
> *moment. She saw it now in just the same way; not*
> *remembering going into the garden or any end to being*
> *in the bright sun between the blazing flowers, the two*
> *banks linked by the slowly swinging bees, nothing else*
> *in the world, no house behind the little path, no garden*
> *beyond it. (II, 213)*

Contrasted with other scenes in childhood, "whole pieces of life indoors and out, coming up bit by bit as one thought, but all mixed with sadness and pain and bothers with people" (II, 214), the flower-alley scene, frequently repeated in different chapter-volumes, represents a return to the first moment of consciousness, a moment of innocence, before the ambivalence, the yearnings, or the separation of mind and body began.

In adulthood, Miriam has to suffer these contradictory impulses. Her longing for manly independence and intellectual vigor conflicts with her need to be recognized as a woman, her appreciation of feminine sensitivity, and her oceanic feelings of simultaneity and wonder.

The ambivalence affects her view of herself as a woman and her performance as a musician, if not a writer. She judges herself harshly:

> *She had no right to her understanding of music; no*
> *business to get away into it and hide her defects and*
> *get out of things and escape the proper exposure of her*
> *failure. In a man it would have been excusable. . . . This*
> *dingy woman playing with the directness and decision*
> *of a man was like some strange beast in the room.*
> *(II, 335)*

Various people tell her to continue her painting, her music, her writing. A palmist at Newlands tells her: " 'Whatever you do, write. If you haven't written yet, write, if you don't succeed go on writing' " (II, 129). This same palmist says Miriam's self-confidence is broken. Miriam admits, " 'I used to be self-confident and was so no longer. It's true' " (II, 129). That her lack of self-confidence can be attributed to her ambivalence concerning her sexual identity seems highly probable.

As a result of her brief identification with women, she sees them as "strained and defaced, all masked watchfulness, cut off from themselves, weaving romances in their efforts to get back ......." (III, 205). But, having seen this reality, she ponders, "But what was the *use* of not being deceived?" (III, 205). However, she sees no way to expose sham behavior in all of humanity, and she does not know how to escape masking and hiding "without surrendering life itself, treacherous countenancing of the fiendish spectacle" (III, 205).

Tired of wandering in this maze of human relationships, she muses over her ability to be suddenly thrilled by existence per se:

> *A future without prospects, the many doors she had tried, closed willingly by her own hand, the growing suspicion that nowhere in the world was a door that would open wide to receive her, the menace of an increasing fatigue, crises of withering mental pain, and then suddenly this incomparable sense of being plumb at the centre of rejoicing. (III, 288)*

But it is "plumb at the centre" of this labyrinth where her isolated room and her writing pad are located, that she also sees herself as a monster, rejecting reverence and affluence as a wife, and insisting on her independence as a writer. Returning alone to that room one evening, she identifies with a pitiful creature in an alleyway:

> *Within it was the figure of an old woman bent over the gutter. Lamplight fell upon the sheeny slopes of her shawl and tattered skirt. Familiar. Forgotten. The last, hidden truth of London, spoiling the night. She quickened her steps, gazing. Underneath the forward-falling crushed old bonnet shone the lower half of a bare scalp . . . reddish . . . studded with dull, wartlike knobs. . . . Unimaginable horror quietly there. Revealed. Welcome. The head turned stealthily as she passed and she met the expected sidelong glance; naked recognition, leering from the awful face above the outstretched*

*bare arm. It was herself, set in her path and waiting*
*through all the years. Her beloved hated secret self,*
*known to this old woman. (III, 288)*

The adjectives ''beloved'' and ''hated'' indicate the ambivalence she
feels toward her socially-aberrant self. Though she enjoys the company
of others, she would quickly forsake them were she to lose her freedom
by cultivating friendships, by giving herself over to a man, or by
serving a religion that forced her to stop thinking. Feeling that her
music and writing are useless to this world, she believes that no one
cares about her. She is alone and unjustified:

> *I am left in a corner with death. But it is I who am left,*
> *and not dead. .......*
>
> *Greater than the sadness of not being good, more*
> *thrilling, was the joy of feeling ready to take responsi-*
> *bility for oneself.*
>
> *I must create my life. Life is creation. Self and circum-*
> *stances the raw material. But so many lives I can't*
> *create. And in going off to create my own I must leave*
> *behind uncreated lives. (III, 507-08)*

This passage is crucial to the *Künstlerroman*. In it, Miriam voices the
despair of any sensitive artist who would like to experience life in all its
forms and also to create that experience anew on palette, instrument,
or pad.

However, Miriam also bemoans the specific tensions which arise in
women's lives--to be the muse, the angel, the nurse, the hostess, the
career-woman, the mother, the Venus, or the lover--simultaneously.
Because few women can excel at all the things they are expected to do
and be, Elizabeth Janeway claims, ''The effect of the split in women's
traditional role . . . is to direct women toward flexibility rather than
single-mindedness, toward responsiveness rather than decisiveness,
and toward the acceptance of themselves they live with as a bit
inadequate.'' [10]

117

Miriam searches for the outlet she needs, the right balance between the ideal woman and the ideal artist. The artist must devote herself to one talent; the ideal woman traditionally is capable of doing many things. Miriam is propelled toward her goal of writing, despite her revulsion for the unacceptable solitary life, the lack of moral support, and the steadfastness it takes to write. Defending this choice to a male friend, she asserts, " 'There's more space within than without' " (IV, 168).

That insistence on self-knowledge indicates progress toward individuation, an ability to assert and to recognize her identity in whatever background she finds herself, and a growing sophistication. But that growth interacts with a stable picture she has of herself, a moment of perfection:

> *This person who had stood for the first time alone upon the sunlit garden-path between the banks of flowers and watched them, through the pattern made by the bees sailing heavily across from bank to bank at the level of her face, and wondered at them all, flowers and bees and sunlight, at their all being there when nobody was about, and had looked for so long at the bright masses, and now could re-see them with knowledge of their names and ways and of the dark earth underneath, and, still, just as they were in that moment that had neither beginning nor end ....... this person ....... was the one who had gazed for ever at the flower-banks, unchanged. (IV, 177-78)*

A woman who experiences that unison of now, past, here, there, and its totality fits the traditional view of the receptive, unconscious, sensitive receptacle, woman. By contrast, a person who directs her life to achieve one goal is aberrant. Indeed, Miriam believes that such a woman has to be trained to think differently and is a freak (III, 393). Miriam is living by ideas that do not change rapidly. To create one thing is to leave others uncreated--in effect, destroyed. Because they internalize the concept of females as nurturant and receptive and because art entails destruction, women react sensitively to the message that comes from so many quarters: "Women can't write. Can't paint."

118

Miriam sidesteps the issue by claiming to be a man, at least in her desire for solitude and in her sinful joy in contemplation: "But from the human atmosphere all about her came the suggestion that this retreat into the centre of her eternal profanity ....... was an evasion whose price she would live to regret" (IV, 299).

Her ambivalence is part of her being. She enters the magic circle of her lamp and withdraws beyond the alleyways, the boundaries, which restrict her. But in order to find that light, she has, paradoxically, to descend into the dark maze of her life, down to the "changeless central zone of her being" (IV, 299).

> *With a sense of battle waged, though still all about her ....... was the chill darkness that yet might prove to be the reality for which she was bound, she drew back and back and caught a glimpse, through an opening inward eye, of a gap in a low hedge, between two dewy lawns, through which she could see the features of some forgotten scene, the last of a fading twilight upon the gloomy leaves of dark, clustered bushes and, further off, its friendly glimmer upon massive tree-trunks, and wondered, as the scene vanished, why the realization of a garden as a gatherer of growing darkness should be so deeply satisfying, and why these shadowy shrubs and trees should move her to imagine them as they would be in morning light. And why it was that only garden scenes, and never open country, and never the interiors of buildings, returned of themselves without associative link or deliberate effort of memory. (IV, 299-300)*

The garden is, of course, her first conscious memory. The growing darkness reflects the loss of gaiety connected with solitude, the awareness of closures she will have to make in order to maintain her independence, and the darkness she connects with her own "evil genius." Rebirth requires responsibility for the offspring. The burden entails a loss of peace, if not of innocence.

Despite this attraction for the dark and peaceful garden, Miriam still longs for the light of the earlier one, which will always exist in her memory and will always appeal. She attends a Quaker meeting in the attempt to recreate that same beauty. She labors at the meeting house,

> *down through the layers of her surface being, a familiar process. Down and down through a series of circles each wider than the last, each opening with the indrawing of a breath whose outward flow pressed her downward towards the next, nearer to the living centre. Again thought touched her, comparing this research to a kind of mining operation. For indeed it was not flight. There was resistance from within* ....... *(IV, 498)*

This resistance is connected with her inability to accept the "evil genius," the narcissism, necessary for individuation and for art. She realizes a fact of human nature and, as I see it, a cause of women's inability to devote themselves unconditionally to art: "We are perambulating Judgment Days....... If one could fully forgive oneself, the energy it takes to screen off the memory of the past would be set free" (IV, 607).

The barriers she sees in life--financial instability, unprofessional training, acquaintances who challenge her way of life, bars at windows, drunkards standing in her pathway, people who prejudge her limitations--all these are merely shadows cast in the garden compared to the barriers she erects internally by accepting imposed standards of womanly behavior. The flower of womanhood forms the banks of her pathway. Only by circuitous mining, by contemplation, can she transform the babe in the garden into the artist/woman who is qualified to be the heroine of *Pilgrimage*. She eventually learns: "Contemplation is adventure into discovery; reality. . . . Fully to recognize, one must be alone. Away in the farthest reaches of one's being. As one can richly be, even with others, provided they have no claims. Provided one is neither guest nor host" (IV, 657). The trick is to find people who are willing to accompany one on the same basis. But even among friends, she loses touch with them as people and with herself as a woman whenever she writes. She has learned: "To write is to forsake life. Every time I know this, in advance. Yet whenever something comes that sets the tips of my fingers tingling to record it, I forget the price; eagerly face the strange journey down and down to the centre of being" (IV, 609).

120

# THE SONG OF THE LARK

Whereas Miriam comprehends that her art creates a death from which there is a rebirth of sorts, Thea Kronborg, in *The Song of the Lark* (1915) believes that her art is the only form of life. Thea's journey takes the form of a refinement, a husking of all but the essence. Her artistic life truly begins when she moves into a separate wing of her parent's house. But her "genius" is something alien to her then:

> She knew, of course, that there was something about her that was different. But it was more like a friendly spirit than like anything that was a part of herself. She brought everything to it, and it answered her; happiness consisted of that backward and forward movement of herself. The something came and went, she never knew how. (p. 100)

When she gets the opportunity to study in Chicago, she leaves with a little more confidence, but not much: "She was all there, and something else was there, too--in her heart, was it, or under her cheek? Anyhow, it was about her somewhere, that warm sureness, that sturdy little companion with whom she shared a secret" (p. 199). She is a divided being, unsure of herself as an artist, dependent upon an uncontrollable influx. Her teacher reminds her, " 'Every artist makes himself born. It is very much harder than the other time, and longer' " (p. 221).

Determined to give birth to this artist, she works diligently, willing to make it happen. But Harsanyi informs her: " 'The voice is a wild thing. It can't be bred in captivity' " (p. 258). He knows that she wants to be an artist, but she has been working with the wrong instrument, a piano instead of her voice. He also knows that she needs to emerge fully, not keep secret a part of herself. He says, " 'When you find your way to that gift and to that woman, you will be at peace' " (p. 265).

Working with another teacher, Thea comes to realize: "Her voice, more than any other part of her, had to do with that confidence, that sense of wholeness and inner well-being that she had felt at moments ever since she could remember" (p. 272). Having kept this part of herself secret for a very long time, she considers it a separate, second self: "How deep they lay, these second persons, and how little one knew about them, except to guard them fiercely" (p. 273). It is this self she needs to join in order to give birth to one human being.

When she returns home for a visit to friendly soil, the germination process begins. The country generously gives "its joyous force, its large-hearted, childlike power to love . . ." (p. 277). This same feeling of openness is evident in "The Song of the Lark," a painting which also satisfies her. Once again at home, she returns to her room as though she were an embryo, dreaming dreams "in a little morning cave" (p. 300). But to return to the original womb is impossible. The family atmosphere at home is suffocating. She cannot practice: "There was something in the air that froze her throat" (p. 309). She emerges from her trip knowing that she cannot go back as an integral part of the family. She must shuck this husk in order to go more deeply and eventually to reach the artist within.

She goes back to the city determined to develop her gift, "the treasure of creative power" (p. 333). She has difficulty protecting, let alone developing it, until Philip Frederick Ottenburg offers her a respite in cliff-dweller ruins. These caves truly fertilize. Here, she goes back to a source beyond family, back to the "noble unconsciousness" of Indian dwellers. She converts the power to think "into a power of sustained sensation" (p. 373). All that she feels takes root in "her subconscious self" (p. 374). In ancient pools, she dips into her own psyche and into the ancient rituals: "Thea's bath came to have a ceremonial gravity. The atmosphere of the canon was ritualistic" (p. 378). In this setting, she begins to pull together separate entities, to give birth to a whole artist:

> *Here everything was simple and definite, as things had been in childhood. . . . The things that were really hers separated themselves from the rest. Her ideas were simplified, became sharper and clearer. She felt united and strong. (p. 380)*

But separating and refining become difficult feats. "The persistent affirmation--or denial" that she feels may be the affirmation of the artist and the denial of the affiliative needs she had earlier felt. She has been able to shed parental guidance for "older and higher obligations"

(p. 383). She is able to dismiss Philip's suggestion of marriage. Having given birth to her artistic soul, she wants only her strength, talent, and independence.

She travels to Berlin, where she can study the German language and the innuendoes that she needs for opera. As Fred says, "It will be almost like being born again" (p. 464). Each time she nourishes her art, she moves further and farther, in training and in distance, from her biological mother. Though she has some doubts, some need to feel safe within that family, she goes forward to what Dr. Archie realizes is her "original want" (p. 488), formed in early youth.

To give birth to the artist-self within, she must deny her biological mother and her affiliative needs. The daughter gives way to the artist. In order to express, she has to forego pleasures she enjoyed as a child. She can draw upon her early childhood pleasures for refreshment; she can recall the joy of waking as a "precious self," but she has refined the twofold person, child and artist, into artist. Ironically, in giving birth to the artist, she has reduced the whole to the essence. As Thea says, "A child's attitude toward everything is an artist's attitude. I am more or less of an artist now, but then I was nothing else" (p. 551). The spontaneous artistic perception of the child changes to the willed refinement of the adult artist. The narrator explains, "Artistic growth is, more than it is anything else, a refining of the sense of truthfulness. The stupid believe that to be truthful is easy; only the artist, the great artist, knows how difficult it is" (p. 571).

To go forward, Thea has had to journey to the interior, to the uterine room in her family's house, to the womb of a canon cave and bath, and to the beginnings of a new speech, the language of Wagnerian opera. In giving birth to the artist, she paradoxically exhibits and loses her womanhood on stage. Her life becomes an abstract, impersonal one where "womanliness," as defined by society, is unessential and where artistry is all.


## MARY OLIVIER: A LIFE

In May Sinclair's *Mary Olivier: A Life* (1919), the heroine also refines her existence to evoke the abstract and the impersonal. Furthermore,

123

on her journey to the interior, she rationalizes a willed rather than a sacrificial loss of desire, selfishness, and personality.

In her early childhood, Mary feels in the open air a physical joy, a happiness mixed "with the queer light and with the flat fields and the tall, bare trees" (p. 50). She calls these moments "her secret happiness" (p. 94). When, as a teenager, she reads Spinoza, she explains, "Thinking about him--after the Christian God--was like coming out of a small dark room into an immense open space filled with happy light" (p. 100). This light shines with her for many years. She tries to talk with an aunt about pantheism, but the woman fears reprisals from the family if she discusses unorthodox philosophy. As a result,

> Mary saw that she was likely to be alone in her adven-
> ture. It appeared to her more than ever as a journey
> into a beautiful, quiet yet exciting country where you
> could go on and on. The mere pleasure of being able to
> move enchanted her. But nobody would go with her.
> (p. 109)

Most of all, she fears telling her mother. Her father reminds her of Jehovah, a far cry from Spinoza's vision of the ultimate.

Eventually, she finds travel mates in Shelley and Plato. She also finds refuge in a tiny room set aside for her, a room too small for anyone else. There, she can look at the natural scenes and read the things that make her happy. Those very things disconcert Mrs. Olivier, who challenges Mary's unbelief. Mrs. Olivier chides: "Self-will has been your beset-ting sin ever since you were a little baby crying for something you couldn't have. You kicked before you could talk" (p. 169). The ensuing dialogue between mother and daughter is one that Mary continues with herself throughout adulthood. Mary argues:

> "I can't help it if the things I think of make me happy.
> And you don't know how nice it feels to be free."

> "Precious freedom!--to do what you like and think what
> you like, without caring."

*"There's a part of me that doesn't care and there's a part that cares frightfully."*

*The part that cared was not free. Not free. Prisoned in her mother's bedroom with the yellow furniture that remembered. Her mother's face that remembered. . . . And her own heart, sinking at each beat, dragging remembrance. A dead child, remembering and returning. (p. 170)*

The dead-child metaphor is apt. For Mary gives birth again and again to this dead child, this caring child who must negate her self-interest in order to win the approval of those she loves. To develop as an artist, she must develop an independent personality, but to be a woman she must be unselfish.

Chafing under the conflict, she is driven by pent-up energy to play the piano wildly; her mother asks her not to play like that, because she can be heard all over the village. She rebels, continuing to play, but her hands stiffen and she forgets the notes. She rushes out, to see all around her, "Stone walls. A wild country, caught in the net of the stone walls" (p. 178). She charges out farther, to the moors and the hills that were free: "They had slipped from the net of the walls" (p. 178).

Mary, too, devises a way to escape from the net of her parents. She is expected to bridle her will to make their lives more comfortable. Despite a heart that beats more quickly whenever she thinks of the piano, she realizes:

*She would never play well. At any minute her father's voice or her mother's eyes would stiffen her fingers and stop them. She knew what she would do; she had always known. She would make poems. They couldn't hear you making poems. They couldn't see your thoughts falling into sound patterns. (p. 184)*

Thus, Mary's private journey becomes quieter and more introspective.

At a party in someone else's home, she makes her hosts and herself happy by playing the piano. She is interrupted by news that her alcoholic father has died. With a biting, aching madness, she feels guilty about having played the piano while her father was dying: "She hated the conceited, happy self that hadn't cared" (p. 192). Although she still longs to play, and even furtively and soundlessly runs her hands over the keys at a later date, "She was ashamed as if the piano were tempting her to some cruel, abominable sin" (p. 199). Mary has had to give birth once again to the dead child, the one who cares and wants to be loved.

She seeks refuge in the German philosophers and poets. In daydreams of a romance with a new acquaintance, Maurice Jourdain, she can be happy only by imagining self-immolation and a rebirth in his existence, "to live his exciting, adventurous, dangerous life" (p. 227). Her own life becomes a secret, willful, and therefore supposedly sinful one of writing poems. Yet she still believes that crushing anyone's real, secret self, as her mother would like to do, is sinful, too. In discussing will and conscience with a neighbor, she realizes that her conscience may be nothing more than her mother's and her grandmother's consciences. Listening to Mr. Sutcliffe's warning, "Find out what you want, and when you see your chance coming, take it" (p. 258), she cannot imagine ever being able to get away from the nets that have ensnared her.

Offered the only thing she has expressed a desire for--a trip to Agaye--she feels torn between two desires when her brother falls ill and needs her care. She prays to the "Anything" that might help her: "If Anything's there--make me give up going. Make me think about Roddy. Not about myself. About Roddy. *Roddy*. Make me not want to go to Agaye" (p. 260).

Emerging from the prayer with a sense of security, clarity, and joy, she is pleased not to want to go. She has willed selflessness. The training she has received as a child has finally taken. The dead child is reborn. She foregoes fulfilling her one ambition in order to satisfy her associative needs and to assure her "good-girl" identity.

The impulse toward self-immolation in order to receive love and approval is a common experience among females--artists or non-artists. The appeal of the mythic woman, the patient Griselda, the handmaiden of the gods, is strong. The drive toward self-immolation is counter-productive for the person striving to achieve.

126

To direct oneself toward a single goal one must not only feel justified in doing so, but must also choose a specific target. Like many women, Mary has had some difficulty in choosing. She says: "When I'm making music. I think there's nothing but music in all the world; . . . when I'm writing verses I think there's nothing but writing in all the world; and when I'm playing tennis I think there's nothing but tennis in all the world" (p. 284). Mary's pluralism is typical of the talented female in particular and women in general, who are expected traditionally to play many roles simultaneously.

Mary's choice of writing as an emotional outlet is also based on multiple needs: to assert herself and yet be unobtrusive, to be independent and yet selfless. For her, writing seems to be the least objectionable to others. In addition, writing promotes a feeling of happiness not quite like the pantheistic ecstasy that she felt as a young girl:

> But that ecstasy and this happiness had one quality in common; they belonged to some part of you that was free. A you that had no hereditary destiny; that had got out of the net, or had never been caught in it.
> (p. 312)

Mary has independently given birth to a self that writes. Although still subject to conflicting emotions, she has successfully created what she calls "illusions." She decides to try publishing, to get over the fear "that if somebody reads them the illusion they've created would be gone" (p. 313). She identifies these poems as part of her secret self.

But Mary simultaneously begins reading the New Testament and developing an interpretation of that hidden self as God, her Saviour. She becomes Virgin Mary, creating a divine being--her secret self.

A scholar enters as love-interest and complicates the scene. The need for sexual love is strong. But her mother has a stroke. Mary the daughter plays tug-of-war with Mary the lover; both team up against Mary the artist. The dead child wins. Mary wills her mother to live.

Entering a trance, Mary feels that it is somewhat different from the last one: *"This* is an awful feeling. Dying must be like this" (p. 351). Mary experiences dissolution:

> *Going and coming back; gathered together; incredibly free; disentangled from the net of nerves and veins. It didn't move any more with the movement of the net. . . .*
>
> *Then it willed. Your self willed. It was free to will. You knew that it had never been free before except once; it had never willed before except once. Willing was this. Waves and waves of will, coming on and on, making your will, driving it through empty time. . . .*
> *. . . . . . . Time where nothing happens except this. Where nothing happens except God's will. God's will in your will. Self of your self. (p. 351)*

Her mother gets better, but Mary has nightmares about taking care of "a body without a mind" (p. 352) and eventually develops heart disease, "the net of flesh and blood" snaring a part of her body. After a brief affair with her lover, she is able to will away her desire. Subsequently her mother dies; her lover marries someone else. Looking for a stable reality, Mary turns to nature: "She saw that the beauty of the tree was its real life, and that its real life was in her real self and that her real self was God" (p. 373). The logical conclusion then follows:

> *God's will was your fate. The thing was to know it and not waste your strength in the illusion of resistance.*
>
> *If you were part of God your will was God's will at the moment when you really willed. . . . When you lay still with your eyes shut and made the darkness come on, wave after wave, blotting out your body and the world, blotting out everything but your self and your will, that was a dying to live; a real dying, a real life. (p. 377)*

Wanting things, people, and thoughts had kept her from this beautiful death-in-life, life-in-death. She realizes in her introspective journey that perfect happiness "had not come from the people or the things you

128

thought it had come from, but from somewhere inside yourself" (p. 378). People, places, and things bring happiness only when they become a part of oneself. The self, then, brings happiness.

The necessarily-long quotations show the circuitous route which Mary takes back to the pantheistic joy of childhood, a joy which makes her feel a part of all her surroundings yet free from parental influence. She has resurrected the dead child, the young girl who needed the love of her mother and of her Jehovah-like father. In the darkness, lying still, blinded to concrete reality, she equates God and her own will and thereby justifies her writing, which she and her mother considered to be willful. She becomes both Jehovah and the Mother Mary; the child she brings into the world is dead to the reality of place, time, and person. By negating her desire for these particulars and thus by escaping their nets, Mary feels whole. However, Mary also escapes the particulars needed to convince her readers that this artist is a person and not an abstract will emanating from ethereal realms. The child babbles, the prophet speaks, but the artist disappears.


## ORLANDO

Unlike Sinclair's realistic novel, Virginia Woolf's *Orlando* (1928) depicts the fantastic development of an artist. The protagonist does journey into the interior, but the voyage is an unrealistic one which questions the nature of man and woman as well as the nature of the narrator's self and art.

The fantasy distorts time, quickly moving the hero-ine from 1586 to 1928. Particularly interesting is the hero-ine's change of sex, for "Orlando was a man till the age of thirty; when he became a woman and has remained so ever since" (p. 139). His switch in sex parallels the development of many female achievers, who are tomboys until puberty. According to Dr. Cohen, "After that time, the pressures for traditional femininity, prettiness, ladylike behavior, and apparent passivity in courtship become very strong."[11] As a man, Orlando insisted that women be "obedient, chaste, scented, and exquisitely apparelled" (p. 156). As a woman, she realizes that women are none of these things by nature, "They can only attain these graces, without which they may enjoy none of the delights of life, by the most tedious

129

discipline" (p. 157).Woolf does more than hint, here, that certain differences in the sexes occur through culturalization and that the woman is condemned to insignificant activities in order to obtain other pleasures; the artist, perceiving this fact, circumvents some of these restrictions through imaginative writing.

Orlando journeys not only forward through 340 years, but deep into her person. Chafed by the restraints put upon her as a woman, she grows restless and searches the castle. Descending to the crypts of her ancestors, she "reviewed, as if it were an avenue of great edifices, the progress of her own self along her own past. . . . Slowly there had opened within her something intricate and many-chambered, which one must take a torch to explore, in prose not verse . . ." (p. 175). Women's bodies are complicated; their lives diffuse; and their journeys subject to the detours found in mazes.

Despite the fact that neither her desires nor her interests have changed, the female Orlando gradually becomes more modest of brains and more vain of looks, the longer she is exposed to society. Examining the difference, the narrator suggests that clothing may transform human beings. On the other hand, "clothes are but a symbol of something hid deep beneath. It was a change in Orlando herself that dictated her choice of a woman's dress and of a woman's sex" (p. 188). As startling as this statement may have seemed in 1928, the reader aware of the transsexuals of the seventies pauses to consider. Attitudes are known to change hormonal output; amenorrhea, for instance, usually has a psychological base. What, then, is the true nature of one's sexual identity? The poet, dredging the tunnel of the past, asks such questions about the nature of her sex and its effect upon her artistic output.

Donning the clothing first of one and then of the other sex, and delighting in physical pleasure with both, she experiences life to the fullest. As a result of living through so many external changes in time, place, and sex, she is able to perceive the center, that which remains constant. The Victorian era brings an end to her jaunts, however: "Love, birth, and death were all swaddled in a variety of fine phrases. The sexes drew further and further apart. . . . The life of the average woman was a succession of childbirths" (p. 229). From bawdy to dowdy, woman changes according to the era. Orlando looks back on the radical differences: "Yet through all these changes she had remained, she reflected, fundamentally the same. She had the same brooding meditative temper, the same love of animals and nature, the same passion for the country and the seasons" (p. 237). Knowing that she is the same capable creature, regardless of circumstances, she nevertheless ceases to be able to write; external pressure stills her pen or makes it run, willy-nilly. She feels compelled to purchase a wedding band. The narrator explains, and in so doing, states succinctly one premise of the author: "We write, not with the fingers, but with the whole person. The nerve which controls the pen winds itself about every fibre of our being, threads the heart, pierces the liver" (p. 243). The narrator also warns the writer that spirit and age, free will and determination, are strangely interrelated. Those who try to break the conventions of their time will probably be beaten down, whereas those who flow with the time are, obviously, more readily accepted. Women who lead unconventional lives as artists may expect to be alienated by or exiled from society.

In perceiving the changes and the constants in her behavior as well as the changes in the social milieu, Orlando is aware that the twentieth century heralds a new era:

> *The immensely long tunnel in which she seemed to have been travelling for hundreds of years widened . . . . And so for some seconds the light went on becoming brighter and brighter, and she saw everything more and more clearly . . . . (p. 298)*

The passage resembles a description of the birth canal widening, light pouring in, and consciousness growing. Orlando is more conscious of the self in the twentieth century than in an earlier one. She is giving birth to the conscious female who can publish "The Oak Tree." While focusing on the birth of Orlando the artist, the reader is also reminded of the growing consciousness of women (after partial suffrage in 1918, equal suffrage became British law in 1928). However, the rebirth of this artist, occurring when women were gaining some rights, occurs, too, when Freud was defining them.

The specific reality of a carpenter's ugly finger, lacking a nail, shocks Orlando and prompts introspection:

131

*For the shadow of faintness which the thumb without a*
*nail had cast had deepened now, at the back of her brain*
*. . . into a pool where things dwell in darkness so deep*
*that what they are we scarcely know. She now looked*
*down into this pool or sea in which everything is reflect-*
*ed--and, indeed, some say that all our most violent*
*passions, and art and religion are the reflections which*
*we see in the dark hollow at the back of the head when*
*the visible world is obscured for the time. (p. 323)*

Under the influence of the Freudian shadows, Orlando imaginatively transforms the trees, bushes, and sheep around her "so that with this mixture of truth and falsehood her mind became like a forest in which things moved; lights and shadows changed, and one thing became another" (p. 323).

Having succumbed to Freudian ideas and the symbolist movement in literature, Orlando manifests the interaction between internal and external forces operating on the writer. The dispersal of Freudian ideas allowed writers to express the hitherto inexpressible but also confined them by explaining their art as stemming from sexual repression. Females were released from some sexual restrictions during the influx of these ideas but also smothered by the concept of anatomical destiny. Reacting to these restrictions, Virginia Woolf creates a fantasy that is actually a record of what Orlando (or Virginia Woolf) sees reflected in the pool at the back of her brain, which stores the history of women, the world, and the myths belonging to both. The myths frequently clash with reality; fantasy is one way to transform both.

A female artist who can overstep the boundaries of sex, time, and monetary limitations is obviously unreal. The tale ends at midnight, the magic disperses, and the reader is left in one of the most self-conscious, sex-conscious, and time-conscious eras in history--the twenties. Although this work may not be like the Fascist poem Virginia Woolf described as "a horrid little abortion such as one sees in a glass jar in the museum of some country town,"[12] it does seem suitable to decorate a glass curio-cabinet. With *Orlando,* Virginia Woolf gives birth not to an abortion, not to a breathing babe, but to a marvel, a mechanical android.

# SAVE ME THE WALTZ

More realistic in describing events of the twenties, Zelda Fitzgerald's *Save Me the Waltz* (1932) records a sad interior journey. Futility pervades the imagery and the dialogue of the heroine. Retrospection brings bitterness rather than release.

The novel barely begins before Alabama Beggs lives up to her name by begging, as a child, to be told who or what she was:

> *She wants to be told what she is like, being too young to know that she is like nothing at all and will fill out her skeleton with what she gives off . . . . She does not know that what effort she makes will become herself. It was much later that the child, Alabama, came to realize that the bones of her father could indicate only her limitations. (p. 6)*

Seeing that her father had created the personality of the women in his family by wielding power, Alabama tries to recreate herself. The novel becomes the search for self.

In her youth, many existences seem superior to her caged life at home: "She was at seventeen a philosophical gourmand of possibilities, having sucked on the bones of frustration thrown off from her family's repast without repletion" (p. 26). But the escape that seems most readily available is provided by a man. She tries to give birth to another Alabama Beggs by attaching herself to David Knight:

> *She felt the essence of herself pulled finer and smaller like those streams of spun glass that pull and stretch till there remains but a glimmering illusion. . . . She felt herself very small and ecstatic. Alabama was in love.*
>
> *She crawled into the friendly cave of his ear. (p. 38).*

Describing his ear, "like a mystic maze" (p. 38), Alabama foreshadows the psychological trap that this cave of marriage will become.

The image of spun glass is also pertinent, for she finds herself in a mad whirl wherein she can recreate herself only by molding illusions. She warns an acquaintance: "I am only really myself when I'm somebody else whom I have endowed with these wonderful qualities from my imagination" (p. 70). In retrospect, she sees that mad period in Paris as a time when, playing minor characters, her acquaintances, herself, and her family were all inadequate. Her only escape is to wish herself in David's pocket (p. 116)--into the safety and security of his love. Examining that period, the narrator reflects: "Women sometimes seem to share a quiet, unalterable dogma of persecution that endows even the most sophisticated of them with the inarticulate poignancy of the peasant" (p. 118). Groomed to play multiple and simultaneous roles created by men, a woman senses her inadequacy as a minor character. When Alabama finally decides to dance to her own tune, her muscles are too old and too flabby for serious work.

Although stirred by music to dream of herself as Prometheus or as a faun walking into virgin forests, Alabama perceives that her ballet troupe is a far cry from such grandeur. Their mean activities remind her of "the grovelling, churning movement of insects watched through the sides of a glass jar" (p. 162). Whereas released larvae might be transformed into butterflies, these insects lack the youth and the air required for metamorphosis. Alabama is the star of this ugly troupe, but neither she nor her former rival, Arienne, who dances in "Prometheus," are able to make their way free and clear of the glass jar without injury. Arienne's desperation detracts from her art. In fierce determination, Alabama dances until the glue in her toe shoe infects her blistered feet.

In the hospital, Alabama gives birth to the woman she will be in the future. Her bed and oxygen tent become a tomb, a white cavern, where the air is too easy to breathe. The transfer is like death: "She couldn't feel her body, the air was so light" (p. 193). Like Miriam Henderson's Quaker experience, Mary Olivier's willfull cessation of will, and Thea Kronborg's development of a stage personality, Alabama's convalescence releases her from everyday cares and petty groveling. Refining the impurities of life produces an ethereal, heady realm where the air is easier to breathe but where one is close to death.

She dreams of a clear lake where the vulviform island, phallic poplars, and lush foliage breed tentacular snares and stagnant waters:

*The word "sick" effaced itself against the poisonous air and jittered lamely about between the tips of the island and halted on the white road that ran straight through the middle. "Sick" turned and twisted about the narrow ribbon of the highway like a roasting pig on a spit, and woke Alabama gouging at her eyeballs with the prongs of its letters. (pp. 194-95)*

Alabama's ambition and her subsequent illness are woven into this description and its sexual images, indicating the conflict between her sexual and personal identity. The incompatibility can result in sickness --mental, physical, or imagined. Alabama sports all three kinds. Her self image, when viewed from the vantage point of "womanliness," appears sick, monstrous. To get better, she must leave behind that image by shucking her ambition.

She returns to the protection of her home town:

*It was good to be a stranger in a land when you felt aggressive and acquisitive, but when you began to weave your horizons into some kind of shelter it was good to know that hands you loved had helped in their spinning--made you feel as if the threads would hold together better. (p. 196)*

Arachne the artistic weaver, the spinner of glass, has turned domestic. Challenged by the gods or the powers of life, Alabama wants neither to hang like Arachne nor to turn into a monstrous being like the huge spider. Instead, she gives birth again to the affiliative creature for the attendant warmth and shelter provided. The artist dies; the daughter, mother, wife is born. Alabama, looking into her father's casket, can knowingly remark, " 'Death is the only real elegance' " (p. 203). Compared to the frenzied activity of insects struggling in a glass bottle, death at least *seems* elegant.

The final scene of this novel also suggests introspection. David asks Alabama to stop emptying ash trays before company is well out of the house. She declares the act to be symbolic:

> *"It's very expressive of myself. I just lump everything*
> *in a great heap which I have labelled 'the past,' and,*
> *having thus emptied this deep reservoir that was once*
> *myself, I am ready to continue." (p. 212)*

The emptied, deep reservoir suggests an aborted birth of the artist. The novel is a journey into the interior of the female anatomy where the abortion took place.


## THE GOLDEN NOTEBOOK

Another novel that presents a heroine bent on associative rather than artistic fulfillment, Doris Lessing's *The Golden Notebook* (1962) also takes the form of a journey. The multiplicity and diffusion of the heroine's life are manifest in the several routes the journey takes and the many notebooks the heroine uses to record those separate routes to the interior.

Her journey is hampered by her own awareness of life's barriers: the boundaries of communication, the expressiveness of facts versus the questionable truth of fiction, the crystallizing force of myth versus its power to imprison, the distortion of time on teller and on reader, sexual polarity and its effect on the heroine's literature and life, the self-made barriers against self-exposure, the dryness of form versus the flood of chaos, and the indulgence of naming instead of eliminating problems.

Identifying with artists (of both sexes) who enjoy naming, Anna journeys to the interior, trying to recognize needs and set goals. She thinks back to the Anna who lived the life on which her novel was based,

> *I don't think I really saw people then, except as append-*
> *ages to my needs. It's only now, looking back, that I*
> *understand, but at the time I lived in a brilliantly lit*
> *haze, shifting and flickering according to my changing*
> *desires. (p. 108)*

This journey back is difficult, because the mature Anna who can now reason from a base of broad experience is viewing the younger Anna who seemed not to reason at all:

> *And I get exasperated, trying to remember--it's like*
> *wrestling with an obstinate other-self who insists on its*
> *own kind of privacy. . . . I am appalled at how much*
> *I didn't notice, living inside the subjective, highly-*
> *coloured mist. How do I know that what I 'remember'*
> *was what was important? What I remember was chosen*
> *by Anna, of twenty years ago. (p. 122)*

Time distorts the memory of truth, but time also changes human beings. To the young, the mere accumulation of experience may be more important than the decision-making process or the effects of those events on other lives, ages, countries. The self that exists at this moment differs, though only partially, from the self of the past.

Although this problem of time is the problem of any artist, not necessarily a female, Anna Wulf also suffers the conflict of her personal and sexual identities as she looks back. When she remembers being gloriously happy with Paul, enjoying intercourse in a primitive setting-- at the mouth of a small cave decorated with bushman paintings--the intoxication that Anna felt then horrifies her now because she still longs for that intense feeling. The desire for such dissolution upsets her: "And the 'Anna' of that time is like an enemy, or like an old friend one has known too well and doesn't want to see" (p. 135). The memory heightens the conflict she feels within herself.

The Anna who would like to dissolve in an embrace with Paul is the same Anna who joins the Party on the basis of what Arthur Koestler calls "a private myth" (p. 141). But this Anna is not foolish, impetuous, nor scatter-brained. She knows that, like so many others, she joined the Party feeling a "need for wholeness, for an end to the split, divided, unsatisfactory way we all live. Yet joining the Party intensified the split . . ." (p. 142). She is describing neither a female nor an artist, but a modern human being. However, the conflict she experiences as a woman heightens the fear she has about political submission, dissolution, and abdication from responsibility. After Stalin's death, she understands, "We all have this need for the great man, and create him over and over again [in] the face of all the evidence" (p. 143). In other words, she perceives the human tendency to create myths.

Anna develops a distaste for the fabrications of novels, Communist

137

propaganda, and deceptive Don Juans, with their desire for Earth Mother. She fears the attraction of all myths--in religion, politics, leaders, literature, or sex. If these myths which human beings construct are not true but are based on some irrational longing for appeasement or order, then one should reveal the lies and bare the truth. But her journey has shown that truth is dependent upon perspective. By insisting on private truths, one shatters forms and invites chaos. Anna fears both the appeal of myth and the horror of chaos. A dream metaphorically reveals her tension:

> *I dreamed there was an enormous web of beautiful fabric stretched out . . . . The pictures were illustrations of the myths of mankind but they were not just pictures, they were the myths themselves, so that the soft glittering web was alive. . . . Shaped like a map . . . I stood in a blue mist of space while the globe turned, wearing shades of red for the communist countries, and a patchwork of colours for the rest of the world. . . . The colours are melting and flowing into each other, indescribably beautiful so that the world becomes whole, all one beautiful glittering colour, but a colour I have never seen in life. This is a moment of almost unbearable happiness, the happiness seems to swell up, so that everything suddenly bursts, explodes--I was suddenly standing in space, in silence. . . . The slowly turning world was slowly dissolving, disintegrating and flying off into fragments, all through space, so that all around me were weightless fragments drifting about, bouncing into each other and drifting away. The world had gone, and there was chaos. I was alone in chaos. And very clear in my ear a small voice said: Somebody pulled a thread of the fabric and it all dissolved.* (pp. 256-57)

Like any artist, she is delighted by the metaphor, the crystallization of disparate facts. She tries to state the meaning literally, but her insights quickly fade when her lover moves toward her in his sleep. She thinks: "The truth is I don't care a damn about politics or philosophy or anything else, all I care about is that Michael should turn in the dark and put his face against my breasts" (p. 257). Anna Wulf dislikes being

138

drawn toward artificial order, fears chaos, and escapes into the arms of a lover, where she need neither think nor write. She is re-enacting the kind of dissolution she sees in the world's desire for the great man.

Abhorring irrelevant myths, Anna and her fictional heroine would like to create in life and in fiction a new woman, free, choosing to make her own way in the world. Yet each longs for affiliation with mankind or with one man. Their emotions are still tied to the image of the traditional woman; they have not yet caught up with world conditions. In order to remain free from dependency on men, these women would have to put their work before their relationship to others, or use men for sexual or financial favors. If Anna pulls the thread of the current fabric of her life, if not of the world, chaos will erupt. Its coming prompts both joy and fear--the joy of freedom from externally imposed order and the fear of immolation. Although she refuses to be so destructive, others enjoy destruction. Alone, without the wholeness of love, joy, and communal goals to fill her needs, Anna must rely on intelligence to ward off impending chaos. She feels dry and forced, going through processes of toughening herself in order to meet the difficulties of her new lifestyle.

> *Because she was so tired, because 'the well was dry,' she set her brain on the alert, a small critical, dry machine. She could even feel that intelligence there, at work, defensive and efficient--a machine. And she thought: this intelligence, it's the only barrier between me--... cracking up. (p. 337)*

She believes that human progress is like a well of faith that fills, runs dry, and slowly fills again. Both the world's well and her own have run dry. She needs a source of refreshment to counteract the growing tension, fear, and guilt. Feeling vulnerable and inadequate because her lover has left her, she reacts against the one thing that keeps her from chaos, "this increasingly cold, critical, balancing little brain" (p. 347). The brain is not "feminine." Her lover had disliked it.

In this journey toward the interior of chaos and dry wells, personal and universal, the writer, Doris Lessing, draws the character of writer, Anna Wulf, who draws the character of another writer, Ella, who imagines stories about yet another writer. The compound evasion of

139

self as externally defined is obvious. The flight from myth as a construct for action is also evident. Ella searches for outlines but cannot find in her storehouse of literature (in literary tradition, that is) the kind of creative pattern that will help her. What she sees is only destructive myths.

Fishing among childish dreams or memories of a people is distasteful to Anna, as well. Yet myth is what the modern writer, if not the modern female writer, is forced to use in order to convey meaning to a disparate people. If Anna falls back into myth, as did Joyce, for instance, then she, as woman, is trapped by it, as she has been for centuries, She explains to her psychoanalyst the attraction of myth:

> *'Another bit of chaos rescued and "named." . . . I know the feeling. It's joy. But there's something terrible in it--because I've never known joy, awake, as I do, asleep, during a certain kind of dream-- . . . or when I'm flying like Icarus--during these dreams, no matter what frightening material they incorporate, I could cry with happiness. And I know why--it's because all the pain, and the killing and the violence is safely held in the story and it can't hurt me.'* (p. 402)

Anna knows that if the process of individuation is merely a recognition of various stages of one's life as part of the human experience, and if a person sees them as reflections of archetypal dreams or myths, then she may put away the experience and the individual pain of it (p. 402). But Anna does not want to transform her experiences into myths that have been handed down, because she believes that she's "living the kind of life women never lived before" (p. 403), and she wants to find new ways to express whatever is new in herself. An unconventional *mythos*, however, without a recognizable form, might not find an audience. Society "can't stand formlessness" (p. 406), so people like herself all over the world write away in secret, afraid of what they're thinking (p. 406). She herself fears the formlessness growing in her own life, held together by her intelligence, which is rapidly dissolving because she perceives it as unfeminine and limited. Yet anarchy will reign without that rational power. The tension of this conflict builds.

Anna begins a frightening journey to the interior in a series of nightmares. In the first, an anarchic principle manifests itself in a peasant vase which develops an inhuman personality. Pixie or elf, it unreasonably threatens living things. The second time, the principle takes shape in a dwarf-like old man who "was ugly, vital and powerful, and again, what he represented was pure spite, malice, joy in malice, joy in a destructive impulse" (p. 408). The most frightening nightmare occurs when the uncontrolled force for destruction is embodied in a human being. Anna knows, "I was frightened because if the element is now outside of myth, and inside another human being, then it can only mean it is loose in me also, or can only too easily be evoked" (p. 409).

Men who behave with cruel malice, who embody the principle of joy-in-giving-pain, frighten Anna because they stir her own intellectual curiosity and joyful spite. She dreams of destruction as force, once again:

> *This time there was no disguise anywhere. I was the malicious male-female dwarf figure, the principle of joy-in-destruction; and Saul [her lover] was my counterpart. . . . we were not hostile, we were together in spiteful malice. There was a terrible yearning nostalgia in the dream, the longing for death. We came together and kissed, . . . it was the caress of two half-human creatures, celebrating destruction. (p. 508)*

Her lover is also a writer. In their separate attempts to find order, they create myths to contain chaos and quiet terror. These myths act for the masses in the same way that the dream acts for her; it has the positive effect of resting her. Her psychoanalyst would say that her feeling of release indicates the positive effect of art; in other words, that destruction can generate a creative force. However, in the recognition of her own power for destruction and the need for a matching power which has the potential to dissolve hers, Anna feels self-alienated.

As previously mentioned, one of the most difficult things for women is to assume the role of destroyer. But without destroying--conventions or overused word patterns, for instance--one cannot create, at least not the kind of innovative literature that warrants the reputation of a masterpiece. In addition, there is a tendency to believe that art must come before life in order to deserve the rank of a master work. Tradi-

141

tionally, women respond to life's needs, first. One of Lessing's fictional characters inscribes in a notebook, "A writer is, must be, the Machiavelli of the soul's kitchen" (p. 373). Like most artist-heroines, Anna has difficulty accepting herself as either submissive woman or Machiavellian artist.

She continues to dream, this time about role-playing with Saul, the artist: "I was astonished at how many of the female roles I have not played in life, have refused to play, or were not offered to me. Even in my sleep I knew I was being condemned to play them now because I had refused them in life" (p. 516). In love with Saul, she is created by that writer into a mythic woman of many different roles, roles she and other women are currently trying to refuse in real life, for these mythic women are often impossible angels or repulsive horrors.

After a brief, rollicking session of love-making with Saul, she sits alone, looking down at her naked body, which until now has given her pleasure:

> *I remembered Nelson telling me how sometimes he looked at his wife's body and hated it for its femaleness; he hated it because of the hair in the armpits and around the crotch. Sometimes, he said, he saw his wife as a sort of spider, all clutching arms and legs around a hairy central devouring mouth. . . . My sticky centre seemed disgusting, and when I saw my breasts all I could think of was how they were when they were full of milk, and instead of this being pleasurable, it was revolting. This feeling of being alien to my own body caused my head to swim, until I anchored myself . . . to the thought that what I was experiencing was not my thought at all. I was experiencing, imaginatively, for the first time, the emotions of a homosexual. For the first time the homosexual literature of disgust made sense to me. I realised how much homosexual feeling there is floating loose everywhere, and in people who would never recognise the word as theirs. (p. 524)*

Lessing uses the term *homosexual,* narrowly, to describe the feeling of men who dislike loving women. (For men-hating women, she elsewhere uses the term *lesbian*.) Men who do not love women or who hate them have created images desecrating the female form and personality. Many women, including artists who are particularly sensitive to language and images, have come to accept themselves or their bodies as the horrors depicted in this passage.

Journeying to the interior, Anna the artist grows ever more sensitive to the views of others. Her understanding of a disgust for the female body joins her fear of the ugly anarchic principle it may harbor. Knowing that sanity depends on delight in the sensations of the body as it reacts to surroundings, she moves further away from hers, into a world of delusions, where tigers lurk in the room and curtains become shreds of torn flesh. In a light sleep, she dreams again:

> *I was myself, yet knowing what I thought and dreamed, so there was a personality apart from the Anna who lay asleep; yet who that person is I do not know. It was a person concerned to prevent the disintegration of Anna.*
>
> *As I lay on the surface of the dream-water, and began very slowly to submerge, this person said: 'Anna, you are betraying everything you believe in; you are sunk in subjectivity, yourself, your own needs.' But the Anna who wanted to slip under the dark water would not answer.* (p. 526)

This passage represents Anna's mythical descent to subaqueous realms, particularly to the emotional depths of the unconscious. Anna feels the need to reject the brittle intelligence, to feel "womanly." The dream continues:

> *. . . the sleeping Anna was already just under the surface of the water, rocking on it, wanting to go down into the black depths under her. The admonishing person said: 'Fight. Fight. Fight.' I lay rocking under the water, and the voice was silent, and then I knew the depths of water under me had become dangerous, full of monsters and crocodiles and things I could scarcely imagine, they were so old and tyrannous. Yet their danger was what pulled me down, I wanted the danger.*

*Then, through the deafening water, I heard the voice*
*say: 'Fight. Fight.' I saw that the water was not deep at*
*all, but only a thin sour layer of water at the bottom of a*
*filthy cage. Above me, over the top of the cage, sprawl-*
*ed the tiger. The voice said: 'Anna, you know how to fly.*
*Fly.' So I slowly crawled, like a drunk woman, to my*
*knees in the filthy thin water, then stood up and tried*
*to fly . . . . (p. 526)*

The danger of the tyrannous monsters can be interpreted in many
ways. The myth of the birth of the hero appeals to her. She, too, would
like to fight dragons and emerge victorious. But the dragons and
monsters of the deeps are traditionally females. If she descends to
unconscious levels, must she identify with "clutching arms and legs
around a hairy central devouring mouth"? If she destroys these
dragons, does she become the ugly, dwarfish, anarchic principle? Both
the females of the mythic deep and the active, artistic women who wish
to destroy them appear to be tyrannical. Anna, the intelligent,
independent woman is repulsed by the monstrous, Freudian, mythic
woman who lies hidden in her own psyche. She also rebels against the
anarchic, individualistic id that would selfishly reign.

The intelligent being, believing that escape is possible through reason,
fights dissolution in mythic definitions of women, in sexual urges, or in
destructive anger. The mythic subaqueous realms become "only a thin
sour layer of water at the bottom of a filthy cage"--the remains of a
concept that has caged women for decades, if not centuries. After much
struggling, she escapes and then recognizes the cage as belonging not
to her, but to the tiger, the writer Saul.

Lessing suggests that the male creature is caught in mythic traps.
Psychologists and sociologists have theorized that the myths of the
patriarchal world may be displacement myths. Horney asks: "Is not the
tremendous strength in men of the impulse to creative work in every
field precisely due to their feeling of playing a relatively small part in
the creation of living beings, which constantly impels them to an over-
compensation in achievement?"[13] Whether or not art is the sublima-
tion of id, whether or not the hero dreams of fighting dragon ladies in
order to give birth to himself because he hates his mother or can't
experience the reality of childbirth, are moot points. But Lessing does

not want to see men caught in such traps. She wants male artists not to be caged by subhuman forces, nor caught in their own psyche, nor trapped by social conventions. She wants them, too, to be free spirits, to enjoy their animal vitality, and to create individualistically. Thus, she has Anna warn the tiger to run when people come to cage him.

All the different Annas view this dream, wanting to make a play out of it, but the disinterested, intelligent, objective Anna which had saved her from disintegration says she must stop playing, making stories about life, evading it, but instead must examine scenes from her own life. The controlling personality wants the writer to name events in her life without nostalgia. She dreams again, this time of a projectionist who runs the scenes of her life, both real and imagined:

> *And now it was terrible, because I was faced with the burden of recreating order out of the chaos that my life had become. Time had gone, and my memory did not exist, and I was unable to distinguish between what I had invented and what I had known, and I knew that what I had invented was all false.* (p. 530)

This is truly the journey to the interior, an attempt to re-evaluate without succumbing to the interpretations of others. If women are going to escape the traps of myth and live in the world as it exists, they must rebuild themselves or society. The problem is that women no longer recognize what is their true nature and what has been created by myths. As Karen Horney remarked over fifty years ago:

> *Women have adapted themselves to the wishes of men and felt as if their adaptation were their true nature. That is, they see or saw themselves in the way that their men's wishes demand of them; unconsciously they yielded to the suggestion of masculine thought.* [14]

Both Horney and the fictional Anna realize how difficult it is for women to abandon this heritage. To escape destructive thoughts and roles takes a special kind of courage, Anna thinks:

> *. . . but not the sort of courage I have ever under- stood. It's a small painful sort of courage which is at the*

145

*root of every life, because injustice and cruelty is at*
*the root of life. And the reason why I have only given*
*my attention to the heroic or the beautiful or the intelli-*
*gent is because I won't accept that injustice and the*
*cruelty, and so won't accept the small endurance that is*
*bigger than anything.* (pp. 543-44)

To focus on a "damned blade of grass" (p. 544), that in the aftermath
of bombs pushes through steel debris and the melted crust of the earth,
Anna would have to acknowledge destructive forces as well as the
grass. She cannot commit herself to revere a natural force of life as
opposition to that willful death, though the nurture of her own daughter
has priority in her own life. The thinking Anna longs for a plan to
eliminate the destructive tendency or control it. Looking for such a
rational construct in the newspapers, she finds only words, facts and
statements, unassimilated.

Her final *anagnorisis* is an experience for which there are no words, and
yet she finds it hard to accept the inability to communicate. Searching
inwardly for a diagram to the future, Anna finds no finite plans, only
provisional ones (p. 558), on which she fears to act. More important,
without a blueprint, she decides not to write, for fear of falling into the
trap of artificiality, superficiality, or myth-turned-dogma.

Saul has told her she must write and has even given her the first
sentence of her novel, saying: " 'There are the two women you are,
Anna. Write down: The two women were alone in the London flat' "
(p. 547). *The Golden Notebook* actually begins with these words
suggested by the male writer. However, the novel ends with the two
women entering the mainstream of British life, going their separate
ways: one to marry a wealthy man and the other to mother her child and
to work in social agencies. Both choose to leave art behind. Having
made the journey to the interior, the narrator rejects the demon of her
anarchic principle (her artistic self) and the principle of art as formulated by men; the female narrator prefers to be nurtured or to nurture
others.

# THE BELL JAR

In another odyssey of madness, *The Bell Jar* (1963), Esther Greenwood searches for a way to unite her personal and sexual identity. Cohen explains the difference:

> *As children grow up, they almost seem to have two identities, the sexual one and the personal one. Since the indoctrination as to sexual role comes earliest, beginning in the very first days of life, it tends to color, and at times to overwhelm, the later development of social skills and intellectual capacities.* [15]

*The Bell Jar* is a journey back through divisiveness and an attempt at integration.

Two recurring images suggest the disintegration Esther experiences. A vivid picture of society's condemnation of aberrant behavior occurs on the novel's first page, with a reference to the electrocution of the Rosenbergs. Esther wonders what it would be like to be burned alive; she later experiences the feeling during a faulty shock treatment. This improperly-administered treatment and the controversial execution of the Rosenbergs suggest that molding someone into an acceptable social form can be damaging or fatal.

Alongside the image of being burned alive--seared by society's standards--is the image of being "glassed into infancy," of suffocating in a bell jar. Although Phyllis Chesler uses the phrase to indicate that women prefer to remain children, [16] this dominant image suggests here that women are glassed, molded, bottled, into *having* children. Specifically, Esther feels propelled toward a relationship with the opposite sex. An article she has read warns her: "There was no sure way of not getting stuck with a baby and then you'd really be in a pickle" (p. 89). Esther has seen "a baby pickled in a laboratory jar" (p. 14) and has never forgotten it. By observing, she learns things, and, as she says, "Even when they surprised me or made me sick I never let on" (p. 14). The author suggests that along with the sickening sight of a cadaver which Esther has never forgotten, the pickled baby also disturbs her, perhaps because it reminds her of the role she is expected to play. In addition, it reflects her own suffocated condition, in general.

Her journey to the interior begins when she is "all right again" (p. 4), when she can use lipstick to mask her face effectively and attract men, when she has had a baby and can amuse it with otherwise useless baubles collected during her trip to New York as contest-winner. Looking back, Esther remembers the girl of that summer as a freak (p. 10).

In retracing her beginnings and searching for a self she can accept, she had haunted the cemetery to visit a father who died when she was nine. She felt he had deserted her mother and herself, leaving them both as vulnerable as orphans, wanting love and ill-equipped to help themselves. The trap women face by depending on men is evident. In a suicide attempt, she tries to shed permanently her need for her father and, ironically, gives birth to herself. Feeling like a troll deep inside a basement cavern, she entertains death. Instead, she is found, moaning like a woman in childbirth, deep in this underground chamber. First seeing a slit of light and then bursting through "the thick, warm, furry dark" (p. 193) much like a baby at birth, she is thrust into the world anew, having died and been forcibly resurrected. Unlike the divine or successful hero, she re-enters her original situation; she remains both fatherless and a freak.

During her journey to the interior, whenever she looks into the mirror, she sees herself reflected in an unfavorable light. After a night of drinking and then walking forty-eight blocks, she sees "a big, smudgy-eyed Chinese woman staring idiotically . . . wrinkled and used up" (p. 19). When she bathes, she feels "sweet as a new baby" (p. 22), but is quickly reminded of her "own dirty nature" (p. 25) by Doreen's passing out in a pool of vomit before her door.

At a photographic session of contest winners, she bursts into tears and checks her appearance in a mirror when editors and photographers retreat: "The face that peered back at me seemed to be peering from the grating of a prison cell after a prolonged beating. It looked bruised and puffy and all the wrong colors. It was a face that needed soap and water and Christian tolerance" (p. 114). Feeling alienated from society as a contest-winning poet, she pictures herself as a convict. Instead of baptizing herself with soap, water, and Christian tolerance, she tries to construct a face suitable for public viewing by painting it with cosmetics.

148

Disoriented, suffering shock from an attempted rape, wearing blood on both her cheeks where the woman-hater smeared her, she returns home without removing the dried blood. When she looks in the mirror, she sees only "a sick Indian" (p. 125). She has been initiated; she knows the primitive forces operating against womanhood.

Back home, feeling imprisoned by "the motherly breath of the suburbs" (p. 126) and their escape-proof cages (p. 128), she looks at a photograph she has taken in a booth. She believes that the "dead, black, vacant expression" (p. 164) resembles that in a recent suicide-victim's eyes. The artist within her has died in this world of babies and mothers.

When she herself tries to commit suicide, she gives birth to yet another unrecognizable creature: "You couldn't tell whether the person in the picture was a man or a woman, because their hair was shaved off and sprouted bristly chicken-feather tufts all over their head" (p. 197). Both male and female, she is monstrous--supernatural and inhuman.

Each reflection is freakish--a wrinkled old youngster, a beaten prisoner, a sick Indian, a dead girl, and a newborn monster. Esther can neither accept herself nor find a socially-acceptable identity. In this society that electrocutes its social deviates, she, too, must undergo shock treatment.

Five feet ten, "skinny as a boy and barely rippled" (p. 8), she feels unwomanly, gawky and freakish around men--particularly little ones. She has difficulty identifying with her mother, an unglamorous and non-intellectual woman. Esther looks for models of behavior elsewhere: in Doreen, an intuitive, free-wheeling playboy's "bunny"; in Jay Cee, a brittle editor; in Philomena Guinea, a self-labeled "stupid" millionaire-writer of superficial novels; in a famous poet, a lesbian who cuts herself off from men; in Joan Gilling, a bright girl but a lesbian who hangs herself; and in Dodo Conway, mother of six and a half children. Each model leaves much to be desired. Esther must journey to her own beginnings in order to establish an acceptable sense of self. She feels betrayed by a conceited male psychiatrist who pretended he could help her (much like the betrayal by her father) but who almost electrocutes her. The psychiatrist who eventually plays the role of help-mate on her journey is a woman.

149

Esther relives in therapy the moment when she first saw a baby being born--the day she also saw the hideous, rotting cadaver, and discovered Buddy's hypocrisy, a seeming betrayal by another man. These three images combine to make the wifely role repugnant to her. She cannot imagine that such a life would be anything but dreary for a girl with fifteen years of straight A's. But, despite her personal, academic abilities, society judges her by sexual standards and, therefore, she measures herself by her relationship with men. She follows their advice, even about skiing. She describes her downward spin:

> *I plummeted down past the zigzaggers, . . . through year after year of doubleness and smiles and compromise, into my own past.*

> *People and trees receded on either hand like the dark sides of a tunnel as I hurtled on to the still, bright point at the end of it, the pebble at the bottom of the well, the white sweet baby cradled in its mother's belly.* (p. 108)

The description of the descent on the ski slope suggests a subconscious plunge to the horror that awaited her in the past and to the frustration she feels in the present when recording her journey to the interior as a woman with a baby. This baby has stared out of the glass jar (p. 69), has been taken from a woman moaning in childbirth (p. 72), has threatened from an article in *Reader's Digest* (p. 89), has beamed from the face of Eisenhower, like the "face of a fetus in a bottle" (p. 98), has threatened to erase poetry from her mind and to brainwash her (p. 94), has instilled itself six and a half times in the healthy body of Dodo Conway who nevertheless carts these babies in a hearse-like station-wagon (pp. 149, 163), has threatened from the maternity ward of a hospital (p. 182), has horrified a famous woman poet (p. 248), has hung over Esther's head "like a big stick" (p. 249), and has threatened madness and forced her back to pre-puberty (p. 207) or to being a babe in a glass jar (pp. 209, 267). In summary, Esther has explicitly stated the cause of her madness: "Children made me sick" (p. 131).

Yet the alternatives are unattractive. If she wants to assume the personal identity of a writer, she needs experience about which to write. She lacks even the limited experience usually granted those of her sex, for she's "never had a love affair or a baby or seen anybody die" (p. 135). She tries to do all three before finally being released from the hospital.

The person who dies is not herself, but an old acquaintance and a fellow inmate, a lesbian who finds tenderness and escape in women. Esther describes Joan as intelligent and assertive, "the beaming double of my old best self" (p. 231), a person whose "thoughts and feelings seemed a wry, black image of my own" (p. 246). Esther sees that Joan's battle is similar to her own, although it takes its own direction, in lesbianism. While granting approval to the heterosexual who assimilates the mores of society, institutions of one kind or another have forced this fictional lesbian and others in real life to commit suicide. Although Esther might not choose to avoid heterosexual love, she would like to escape the trap in which such a relationship usually embroils the female.

Temporarily rejecting the necessity of nurturing another being, of committing suicide, or of playing a role created by someone else, she assures herself: "I am. I am. I am." (p. 274). Her identity is determined not through marriage, motherhood, nor an erotic attachment to the male principle. Standing outside these acceptable social structures and seeing only question marks in the future, Esther muses: "There ought, I thought, to be a ritual for being born twice . . ." (p. 275). Since Plath knew of such rituals and even mentioned the rite of baptism in the beginning of the book (p. 22), she suggests the necessity for a new myth or ritual outside existing traditions--a rite for the rebirth of a female artist, herself.

In order to leave the mental institution and escape further searing, Esther must pass before the board, a group of psychiatrists and visitors who will judge her fitness. Guiding herelf by the eyes and faces of her reviewers, "as by a magical thread" (p. 275), she enters the labyrinth of society. If she is not considered an artist and cannot fly to escape the maze, she must follow the guidelines of that social thread. Esther apparently conquers the demon within, accepting the dictum of her reviewers, even to the extent of having a child, of being "all right" again. But she can never forget the sharp corners nor the barriers she has confronted in the maze. As she reflects on the people and events of the past, she says: "They were a part of me. They were my landscape" (p. 267). Esther still fears the suffocation that will force what she calls her "old best self" back into "the bell jar, blank and stopped as a dead baby" (p. 267). The mythic pattern Plath creates is one not of rebirth but of recognition that society does not acknowledge such rebirths for female artists.

The novel seems not only a journey to Esther's interior demons, but a thread to the labyrinth of its author as well. Sylvia Plath's death reminds the reader that barriers in life really can encase or suffocate the artist.


## MRS. STEVENS HEARS THE MERMAIDS SINGING

May Sarton indicates a journey-motif on the first page of *Mrs. Stevens Hears the Mermaids Singing* (1965). Mrs. Stevens, in an aqueous light, wakens "to the illusion that she was swimming up into consciousness from deep water" (p. 11). She spends much of this particular day probing that deep water. Because she is seventy years old, she frequently faces the past, sometimes in opposition--as when her youthful brain exhorts her sluggish body or when she stands beneath a portrait of her younger self. But frequently, when she is working at her desk, the past and present marry in a metaphor crystallized in the interior of her being. On this day, her journeys into the past and the interior, prompted by young journalists who interview her about her methodology and her life, structure this novel.

During her trip through the past, Hilary Stevens reawakens the muse of each book of poetry. She remembers "mining" her first love, Phillippa the governess. She recalls the salon goddess, Willa, whom she adored, eventually conquered, and partially destroyed. She evokes from the past Dorothea, an anti-mystic, a sociologist, and a crucial muse. Whereas Jenny, the young interviewer, says she is tired of being treated as a Medusa (p. 79), Mrs. Stevens believes that the female artist, being a monster, must face herself. She recognized her own personal monsterhood through Dorothea, who had taught her: "If you turn Medusa's face around, it is your own face. It is yourself who must be conquered" (pp. 161-62). Meeting her opposite in Dorothea stirred not only Hilary's love but her anger and then her compassion:

*It was really at first as if they were plunging into a huge exhilarating ocean, as if the very difference in their vision of life gave an enhancing excitement to their meetings. Up to the moment when the anger in Hilary became frightening, frightening to herself. . . . (p. 164)*

This reaction to the scientific detachment, the criticism, and the emotional jealousy of Dorothea provokes Hilary to deal with feelings she had never before released. In her relationship with Dorothea, whose mind is masculine and towering (p. 163), Hilary feels as though the woman in herself, buried since the death of her husband, is born again. She uses the experience both to get in touch with herself and to create poems. She lectures:

*We learn most about ourselves from the unacceptable, from the violent, from the mad one who weeps and roars in the subterranean caves: let this one out into the air and he brings the light with him, the light that has to be earned, the light of compassion for* oneself, *the strange mercy that follows upon any commitment of such depth when it is played out and so has to be faced. (p. 170)*

Falling into the trap of separating the personal and the sexual, Hilary identifies this destructive demon as male, reversing Rollo May's contention that it is female. The encounter with what she perceives as Dorothea's masculine mind has had two different effects, one on her poetry and one on her person. The incident evoked a dry book of poems, argumentative and tough. Hilary realizes, in retrospect, that she was trying to use her mind to lock hard truths. Although she considers the book insignificant, she acknowledges that it is a watershed in her canon.

Trying to explain what she means--that the novel or poem of ideas is not suitable for women, who should strive for wholeness--she is temporarily incapable of communication with any clarity. However, she can explain her continued refusal to grasp power of any kind. She believes that power ends personal freedom for the poet, who "must above all never worry about his effect on other people. . . . Power requires that the inner person never be unmasked. No, we poets have to go naked" (p. 179). She advocates not exhibitionism, but the willingness to be moved and to express that feeling. She personally is moved by women and nourished by men (p. 180).

Having been both nourished by a competitive, intellectual neighbor and stirred by the female ghost of a French villa, she realizes that she has to make peace with herself in a house of her own creation (p. 186). She unconsciously chooses a location with poetic material in the landscape. Ocean and house become symbols for her mother in the next book of poems.

The male interviewer summarizes Hilary's long inward journey with his statement about women's work: "They have to write from the whole of themselves, so the feminine genius is the genius of self-creation. The outer world will never be as crucial for its flowering as the inner world . . ." (p. 196). The interviewer does not mention continual re-creation, another aspect of women's insecurity and their battle with the monsters within. Mrs. Stevens agrees with the peroration, but her journey to the interior continues even after the interviewers leave.

A young protégé finds her in the garden, and a battle of the two poets begins when he tries to dump at her feet the self-disgust he feels over a homosexual encounter with a sailor who has stolen his wallet. He needs to be nourished by her. Hilary tries to convince him that the experience can be useful though uncomfortable.

Whereas Mar believes that poems come out of self-respect, Mrs. Stevens believes self-disgust can just as well be the source of poetry. Everything can be turned into poetry. Unlike Anna Wulf's belief that poetry is an evasion, a way out, Hilary Stevens sees it as a way in, "excruciating self-discipline, the ability to deal with anxiety, . . . the fighting through each time to the *means* toward . . . transposition" (p. 214). She would have Mar transform the experience into poetry, not dump it at her feet to request compassion.

However, he claims that his real desire is more experience: "Danger, excitement, the unknown person--unlike me--conquered by sheer physical need, clean of any feeling except that" (p. 207). Mrs. Stevens reconsiders. Although she has had both homosexual and heterosexual affairs, they have always been prompted by love. She realizes that his hell and hers are different:

154

*"Different because you're a man and I'm a woman, I suppose. I wouldn't get any kick out of a prostitute. But I do know something of the excitement of discovering the unknown, how one feels driven to explore the unknown person, to break down barriers, to understand, to be enlarged, to discover, the tremendous excitement of that kind of conquest. Of course sex is mixed up with it. That's sure. But if it were only sex, it wouldn't be worth the candle. When I get stirred up, it's the whole of me that gets stirred. I can't separate soul and body, don't you see?"* (pp. 208-09)

He wants the separation. She insists, "True feeling justifies, whatever it may cost" (p. 210), but Mar feels devastated by feeling and needs instead action, unchecked.

The difference between this man's and this woman's attitude toward sex and feeling is also a frequent source of conflict in other novels written by females. Michelle Rosaldo, the sociologist, tries to explain some of the forces operating on the sexes:

*Distance permits men . . . to stand apart from intimate interaction . . . . Women's lives are marked by neither privacy nor distance. They are imbedded in, and subject to, the demands of immediate interaction. Women, more than men, must respond to the personal needs of those around them . . . .* [17]

Add to this sociological phenomenon the biological fact that women's erogeneity is more diffuse than men's [18] and that their biosexual experiences challenge boundaries of self and other, [19] and one can understand Mrs. Stevens' willingness "to be enlarged" and to use both soul and body. She accuses Mar of fearing emotion and exposure, "the terrible fear that if you give a fraction of yourself away you are *diminished*" (p. 212).

It may be true, however, that women insist on this necessity for an interrelationship between body and feeling because they have been trained to revere physical sensations only when they are part of a romantic involvement. Literature tells them so. Mothers warn them.

*Reader's Digest* warns them. *Modern Romance* warms their fancy. In her appreciation of the landscape, Mrs. Stevens has romanticized. Seeing a quarry in what she calls "an unreal light," she is reminded of Poussin and wants nymphs nearby to complete the picture. Mar, on the other hand, likes the quarry just as it is (pp. 202-03).

The conflict between the two perambulating artists is set aside momentarily when Mrs. Stevens is absorbed in looking at one quarry:

> *"Odd, isn't it? How these quarries, blasted open by dynamite, the scene of so much violence, so much lifting and carrying too, after they are abandoned, become magic places, deep ponds." (p. 211)*

Arguing once again that the personal quarry is bound to be dry if one separates sex and feeling, she suddenly becomes aware that Mar was the young man she'd dreamed of being when she was his age. Recognizing the father-figure lurking in him, she did not want the boy destroyed. It was the boy in her that wrote the poems and justified her life by looking through immature boy's eyes:

> *She saw that she had been saved a great deal by being a woman, been saved by nature itself from some kinds of degradation and shame, and that she had been saved also by being a mystic of sorts. Transcending, sublimating--these would not be his way. His way would have to deal with gritty substance; the quarry as it was, not seen in a special light. He must not be bound to her wheel of boy and woman and the two married within her to make the poems. His poems would be cramped and distorted if he did not live out his life to the full, as a man. (p. 215)*

Releasing him from her influence to find his own route, she knows that each encounter with others and each farewell bring a new beginning: "Peace, order, and poetry, to be won over and over again, and never for good, out of the raw, chaotic material" (p. 220).

Despite the fact that her journey to the interior provides a means for tapping emotions that would otherwise remain inexpressible, reveals aspects of her personality hitherto hidden, structures a novel, and forms an aesthetic theory, it also reveals the separation of the heroine's personal and sexual identity. Not being able to enter all areas of life freely, she feels incomplete, monstrous, and divided. She confesses: "I would have liked to be . . . a woman with many children, a great husband, . . . and no talent!" (p. 219). She is driven once again to the quarry of her desk.

## SURFACING

The title of Margaret Atwood's novel, *Surfacing* (1972), suggests emergence from sub-realms. That it is also a personal journey is confirmed by the narrator's opening words, "I can't believe I'm on this road again" (p. 9). Searching in the Canadian woods for her lost father, she journeys also to find herself.

She recalls giving up serious for commercial art on the advice of her lover (p. 52). Working on illustrations for a book of folk tales, she draws a princess, looking up admiringly at a golden phoenix (p. 54), the eternal male springing from ruin. The illustration reminds her of her own happy childhood, when she felt like a princess and her father was a god (p. 104). She remembers her school years, when she played the role of victim and learned to become an escape artist (p. 72). But she warns herself to be careful:

> *I have to be sure they're my own and not the memories of other people telling me what I felt, how I acted, what I said: if the events are wrong the feelings I remember about them will be wrong too, I'll start inventing them and there will be no way of correcting it, the ones who could help are gone.* (p. 73)

Slowly retracing her past, she recalls her brother's drowning:

> *His drowning never seemed to have affected him as much as I thought it should, he couldn't even remember it. If it had happened to me I would have felt there was something special about me, to be raised from the dead like that; I would have returned with secrets, I would have known things other people didn't.* (p. 74)

157

Obviously, the heroine has been inundated with tales of mythic heroes--
phoenixes, divine kings, surfaced gods who bring up elixirs, treasures,
or secrets from other gods. Taking direction from males like them, she
has been afraid to ask her teachers questions about morals and motives
in life and in the history that she's been taught. She has accepted the
myths and history of society.

She discovers pictures she and her brother have drawn. Hers are
designed with eggs, rabbits, grass, trees, flowers, the sun, and the
moon. His are covered with monsters, wars, explosion, heroism. She
labels him a realist. Looking through snapshots showing her happy
face, she realizes that she has lost the capacity for feeling:

> *At some point my neck must have closed over . . .*
> *shutting me into my head; since then everything had*
> *been glancing off me, it was like being in a vase . . . .*
> *Bottles distort for the observer too: . . . to them watch-*
> *ing I must have appeared grostesque. (p. 106)*

Examining her old scrapbooks, her father's maps and drawings, she
realizes, "It was no longer his death but my own that concerned
me . . ." (p. 107). Submerging several times in a lake near the face of a
cliff in order to locate Indian drawings, clues to her father's disappear-
ance, she finds his body during a long dive that nearly kills her too.
Resting on the bottom of the canoe, she remembers the form she has
seen. It fills a gap of forgotten time:

> *At first I thought it was my drowned brother, hair*
> *floating around the face, image I'd kept from before I*
> *was born, but it couldn't be him, he had not drowned*
> *after all, he was elsewhere. Then I recognized it: it*
> *wasn't ever my brother I'd been remembering, that had*
> *been a disguise.*
>
> *I knew when it was, it was in a bottle curled up, staring*
> *out at me like a cat pickled; it had huge jelly eyes and*
> *fins instead of hands, fish gills, I couldn't let it out, it*
> *was dead already, it had drowned in air. It was there*
> *when I woke up, suspended in the air above me like a*
> *chalice, an evil grail and I thought, Whatever it is, part*

*of myself or a separate creature, I killed it. It wasn't a*
*child but it could have been one, I didn't allow it.*
*(p. 143)*

Subsequently, she realizes that even that version was imagined. She
had never seen the fetus: "The bottle had been logical, pure logic,
remnant of the trapped and decaying animals, secreted by my head,
enclosure, something to keep the death away from me" (p. 143). Not
willing to accept her guilt, she created a different version of the
abortion, "memories fraudulent as passports" (p. 144).

Surfacing from the depths, she also surfaces from deception. Shocked,
she rejects her own humanity, trying to identify with the natural spirits
that emanate from the island cabin in Indian territory. In the open air,
she has sexual intercourse with her lover, hoping that procreation will
cancel abortion. She burns or breaks all evidence of civilization in the
cabin, including her paints and brushes. Then she baptizes her body:

> *My back is on the sand, my head rests against the rock,*
> *innocent as plankton; my hair spreads out, moving and*
> *fluid in the water. The earth rotates, holding my body*
> *down to it as it holds the moon; the sun pounds in the*
> *sky, red flames and rays pulsing from it, searing away*
> *the wrong form that encases me, dry rain soaking*
> *through me, warming the blood egg I carry. I dip my*
> *head beneath the water, washing my eyes. (pp. 177-78)*

With naturalized vision, she destroys everything to put herself in touch
with nature. She becomes animal, tree, the "thing in which the trees
and animals move and grow, . . . a place" (p. 181). She communicates
with natural spirits.

Having spoken to her parents in their language, she trudges back to the
civilization of her cabin. Perceiving with both heart and mind, she
realizes that the man who betrayed her was an average man: "But I
was not prepared for the average, its needless cruelties and lies. My
brother saw the danger early. To immerse oneself, join in the war, or to
be destroyed. Though there ought to be other choices" (p. 189)

Her journey to mythical realms and unconscious wells releases emotions, wreaks havoc, but supplies neither privileged information nor permanent magical force to the heroine. Having tried the magic of spirits, she realizes that she must eat to live and to bear a child. Having thrown away the tools of her trade while under the spell of magic, she gives no indication that she will return to art. Her future will not include myth-making. In her hopes for a truly human child rather than a divine son, she echoes the wishes of many women who have grown weary in the role of handmaiden to the gods.

But myth-making is a form of flight or invisibility, the only two escapes formerly possible. She had prayed unsuccessfully for invisibility. Flight had proven dangerous to her mother. She recalls a story her mother had told her about making wings from an old umbrella, jumping off the barn roof in an attempt to fly, and breaking both ankles (p. 123). New ways must be invented.

She realizes that in the future she must live without gods, parents, or icons: "defining them by their absence; and love by its failures, power by its loss, its renunciation. I regret them; but they give only one kind of truth, one hand" (p. 189). She realizes that her father had "islanded" his life, trying "to sustain his illusions of reason and benevolent order" (p. 190). Myth-making is but one way to weave artificial order. Her mother had meticulously kept records in a diary, facts "that allowed her to omit the other things, the pain and isolation and whatever it was she was fighting against, something in a vanished history, I can never know" (p. 190).

What, then, does this journey to the interior explain? Of what benefits is a rebirth of the heroine, up from the deeps of earth and lake? Previously, the heroine believed that if she had almost drowned, she would have emerged knowledgeable. This natural woman, spawned by no kingfisher, has a limited vision:

> *This above all, to refuse to be a victim. Unless I can do that I can do nothing. I have to recant, give up the old belief that I am powerless and because of it nothing I can do will ever hurt anyone. A lie which was always more disastrous than the truth would have been. The word games, the winning and losing games are finished; at the moment there are no others but they will*

*have to be invented, withdrawing is no longer possible*
*and the alternative is death. (p. 191)*

The knowledge she has gained from her journey is minimal, even
though the experience provides a source of nourishment, its one
positive effect. But the future is doubtful.

When her lover returns, calling for her, she acknowledges:

> *If I go with him, we will have to talk . . . . For us it's*
> *necessary, the intercession of words; and we will*
> *probably fail, sooner or later, more or less painfully.*
> *That's normal, it's the way it happens now . . . .* (p. 191]

Committed to failure and to an understanding of her part in it, the
narrator has learned, in her journey, her own capacity for destruction
and for self-deception. She has always been aware of her power to give
life.


## FEAR OF FLYING

Many twentieth-century novels of the artist as heroine center on this
*anagnorisis*, this understanding of one's own capability and culpability.
Erica Jong's *Fear of Flying* (1973) is another such novel. It begins
symbolically on a flight to Vienna, with a plane-load of psychoanalysts
returning to commemorate the beginnings of Freudian psychology. The
heroine also journeys back to beginnings; in her psycho-sexual odyssey
she examines what it means to be a woman, what alternatives there are
to presently-accepted womanly roles, who she is, why she is afraid, and
what these questions mean to her writing.

Pondering whether the split image of her mother and herself, both
Terrible and Good, causes her to search for approval, Isadora spends
her life on a quest, supposedly for the man she really wants, but she
admits, "Perhaps the search was really a kind of ritual in which the
process was more important than the end" (p. 110).

The process turns into a query about her need for this man. Despite
"seeing life as contradictory, many-sided, various, funny, tragic, and

161

with moments of outrageous beauty'' (p. 141), she sees herself as some kind of monster. Acknowledging that "women are their own worst enemies" (p. 144), she does not release this guilt by naming it. She berates her cautious good-girl rules one moment (p. 186) and later contradictorily states that she is not a good woman (p. 231). Having been taught the importance of being extraordinary, she longs to be ordinary until she imagines what being ordinary involves. Then the fantasy explodes. In summary, she is a bundle of contradictions.

Her external travels in Europe are less important than her journey to the interior. Filled with wonder at the "terra incognita" of her own brain and its "submerged islands of childhood," the inadequately-explored inner space, she admits:

> It's for this, partly that I write. How can I know what I think unless I see what I write? My writing is the submarine or spaceship which takes me to the unknown worlds within my head. And the adventure is endless and inexhaustible. . . . And each new poem is a new vehicle, designed to delve a little deeper (or fly a little higher) than the one before. (p. 230)

However, her journey to the interior is not only mental but physical. Her sexual odyssey with Adrian provokes fears about disease or pregnancy. She deplores the barriers of the female body:

> The worst thing about being female is the hiddenness of your own body. You spend your whole adolescence arched over backward in the bathroom mirror, trying to look up your cunt. And what do you see? The frizzy halo of pubic hair, the purple labia, the pink alarm button of the clitoris--but never enough! The most important part is invisible. An unexplored canyon, an underground cave, and all sorts of hidden dangers lurking within. (p. 254)

Despite this unflattering but detailed description of the female genitalia, Isadora is puzzled by her body throughout the journey. She fears reprisals there: "Every time I took off my diaphragm I would feel

162

my cervix, searching for some clue. Why did I never know what was going on inside me? Why was my body such a mystery to me?'' (p. 276). No matter how much she peers, her internal organs, so inextricably connected to her behavior, remain unseen. But that does not stop her quest:

> *I tried to examine my physical self, to take stock so that*
> *I could remember who I was--if indeed my body could*
> *be said to be me. . . . One's body is intimately related*
> *to one's writing, although the precise nature of the*
> *connection is subtle and may take years to under-*
> *stand. . . . In a sense, every poem is an attempt to*
> *extend the boundaries of one's body. One's body*
> *becomes the landscape, the sky, and finally the cosmos.*
> *(pp. 311-12)*

This connection between the female body and her writing is crucial. She must accept a body she does not know.

Although her examination of self--her past, her mind, her body-- continues in an on-going process, her most penetrating insights come in the perusal of her writing:

> *I sat down on the bed, spread all my notebooks and*
> *poems around me, and started flipping through a fat*
> *spiral binder which went back almost four years. . . .*
> *everything jumbled together, chaotic, almost illeg-*
> *ible. . . .*
>
> *I flipped pages wildly looking for some clue to my*
> *predicament. . . . God--I had almost forgotten how*
> *miserable I was then, and how lonely. . . . Why should*
> *a bad marriage have been so much more compelling*
> *than no marriage? Why had I clung to my misery so?*
> *Why did I believe it was all I had?*
>
> *As I read the notebook, I began to be drawn into it*
> *as into a novel. I almost began to forget that I had*
> *written it. And then a curious revelation started to*
> *dawn. I stopped blaming myself; it was that simple.*

*Perhaps my finally running away was not due to malice on my part, nor to any disloyalty I need apologize for. Perhaps it was a kind of loyalty to myself. A drastic but necessary way of changing my life.*

. . . . . . . . . . . . . . . . . . . . . . . . . . . . . . . . . . . . . . . . . .

*I went on reading and with each page I grew more philosophical. I knew I did not want to return to the marriage described in that notebook. If Bennett and I got back together again, it would have to be under very different circumstances. And if we did not, I knew I would survive.*

*No electric light bulb went on in my head with that recognition. Nor did I leap into the air and shout Eureka! I sat very quietly looking at the pages I had written. I knew I did not want to be trapped in my own book.*

*It was also heartening to see how much I had changed in the past four years. I was able to send my work out now. I was not afraid to drive. I was able to spend long hours alone writing. I taught, gave lectures, traveled. Terrified of flying as I was, I didn't allow that fear to control me. . . . If some things could change, so could other things. (pp. 313-15)*

This very long passage describing the journey Isadora takes through the record of her life is the crux of the novel. Ironically, the tour through her notebooks takes place in Paris after a driving tour with a lover whose attraction has faded. He has exhorted her to be independent. She admits, "He was, perversely, the instrument of my freedom" (p. 296). But he did not release her from fear. Alone, and unloved, she has felt terror. Her contradictory needs for closeness and freedom have trapped her. Only the written self-examination, read after the driving tour, has given her a clue to the labyrinth of her being. Her external travels were not so vital as the internal journey.

She sleeps and dreams extravagantly of her graduation, her husbands, and of her non-biological mother, a bizarre Colette. The dreams reflect her search for approval in intellectual and physical pursuits, suggest

164

the nourishment available from artists like Colette, who have blazed the trail she follows, and hint at the benefits of being able to love a woman's body. The release of dreaming foreshadows the physical release of blood.

Having expressed philosophically that one's writing is intimately connected with one's body, Erica Jong proves it by describing the vicissitudes of menstruation in a foreign country when one does not have the scientific marvels of pad or tampon. Determined to start anew, Isadora begins the next portion of her journey, childlike, draped in a diaper. Mary Ellman has called menstruation "an image of repeated bankruptcy" [20] and suggested that "the male body lends credence to assertions, while the female takes it away." [21] Isadora supports that notion in identifying the source of her fear. As a teenager, she had suffered amenorrhea and admitted that she was afraid of being a woman:

> Not afraid of the blood . . . but afraid of all the nonsense
> that went along with it. Like being told that if I had
> babies, I'd never be an artist, like my mother's bitter-
> ness, like my grandmother's boring concentration on
> eating and excreting, like being asked by some dough-
> faced boy if I planned to be a secretary. (p. 325)

Having gained some sense of identity from her journals, Isadora can say that menstruation is not only a bankruptcy but a new beginning. Searching for love had been, in effect, a search for self-annihilation:

> I wanted to lose myself in a man, to cease to be me, to
> be transported to heaven on borrowed wings. Isadora
> Icarus, I ought to call myself. And the borrowed wings
> never stayed on when I needed them. Maybe I really
> needed to grow my own. (p. 329)

This growth is symbolically begun in a tub of water. In this pseudo-womb, she examines her body, feeling that something was different: "A nice body. Mine. I decided to keep it. I hugged myself. It was my fear that was missing. . . . Not suddenly. And maybe not for good. But it was gone" (p. 339). She cannot decide what is to become of her marriage or future. Those problems remain for most female artists.

165

Isadora's journey to the interior has taken her back to the womb of a tub, but in her embryonic state she has merely dropped the cloak of fear that she carried in society. Her body and its cycles may encase her in fear once again. But her journals will be a touchstone to remind her of the slow growth that is possible.

## THE ODYSSEY OF KATINOU KALOKOVICH

In another pattern of flight and return to the womb in *The Odyssey of Katinou Kalokovich* (1974), Natalie Petesch describes a fledgling artist's entrapment in a family where she feels unappreciated, her flight, and her subsequent return to the family. In a forthright style that calls upon the symbols of the Judeo-Christian tradition, the narrator charts her inauspicious beginnings and her rites of passage: the delivery on the bathroom floor, the stillbirth blasted into life by air blown from bellows, illness that scars her face and deafens one ear, recognition of second-class citizenship upon the birth of a brother, loss of virginity, defiance of authority, flight from the violent tyranny of her father, marriage for economic reasons, enrollment in art school, escape from marriage, pregnancy resulting from an ill-fitted diaphragm, illegal abortion, escape from death, fatal hunting accident of her lover, act of fellatio forced by her husband, birth of a young sister, institution-alization of her mother, and consequent assumption of the burdens of keeping house and caring for that newborn sister.

The journey is an external one, and all these experiences have but one effect on the narrator's attitude. Whereas the inexperienced and untrained artist hides the tools of her art, the experienced and trained artist uses them to make a frightening portrait of family life and then leaves those tools visible for her own family to see. Although Anna Katinou Kalokovich may be caught in the trap of her sex, her family, her race, her body, and other external forces, her art becomes a state-ment of her unwillingness to succumb and a warning to others. Her tools herald an alternative presently unattainable but no longer unthinkable. She identifies herself as an artist and a potential heroine of the new *mythos*.

# HER MOTHERS

E.M. Broner's novel of the artist depicts yet another journey. The loss of daughter, husband, and chiildhood prompts the heroine of *Her Mothers* (1975) to undertake this odyssey, traipsing across the land-scape of written records, several countries, and her own mental state. Beatrix Palmer, having been to the Holy Land, quarrels with its holiness and with the plastic world that has usurped its power. To establish or affirm her own values, she examines the beginnings of her race, her family, her generation, her sex, her education, marriage, and herself.

During this search, she employs a therapist (a man who traditionally acts as tour-director during such an odyssey) but discovers that he is more a hindrance than helpmate to her writing and her well-being:

> *Beatrix dropped the idea for the book, dropped her doctor, kept her fear of cooking and her daughter, bore her relationships with mother and father, and began a new book.*
>
> *She called it, tentatively,* Unafraid Women, *women who both cooked and lived without fear. She had to go back a long way to find them, about a hundred years for some of them.* (p. 62)

This passage depicts Bea as developing stability and direction. But her insecurity is evident in her procrastination of work on *Unafraid Women*. The narrator remarks: "She is afraid of them" (p. 63).

The vacillation between the bravado of a dragon-slayer and the silence of a hunted animal continues throughout Beatrix's search through the past. She tries to find not only her daughter and her husband, but an acceptable identity which shifts, depending on time, place, and attitude of the beholder. After the cartography of Bea's body, its defects and its assets, the narrator asks the owner, " 'So, you like it?' " Bea answers, " 'No, I hate it' " (p. 82). Bea would like to please others with her looks and thereby please herself. The narrator cautions: "Beatrix will have to learn . . . how not to please. She will have to try to prop herself up on her elbows and not sag. She will have to learn how to greet or to retreat. But not yet. She may never learn all that" (pp. 79-80).

Traveling to Sea Island in her search for literary forebears who will teach her, Beatrix falls sway to the magic of its atmosphere and imagines living there with the plantation's charming but imaginary nineteenth-century master. Novels of the southern tradition and historical romances ensnare many female writers and readers. Literature that feeds the fantasies of masochistic women feeds on women. This vampire attracts Beatrix the woman and tempts Beatrix the writer. She almost succumbs: "Beatrix is ashamed. It is this sensual life that leads her to exploit her own body, to exploit even her mothers" (p. 134). With sympathy for those who suffered in the actual South, she reminds herself, " 'You cannot be your mother; you cannot be your heroine; you cannot be another's color' " (p. 134).

Despite these clear and definite warnings, the heroine's journey takes on the look of self-acceptance if not self-creation. Hunting for clues to her daughter's whereabouts, Beatrix runs across old purses and their mirrors. Searching for Lena, she finds a decrepit bag:

> Bea sees herself in the horizontal row of tiny mirrors, a
> bit of an eye, an arch of brow; next row, the nose; two
> rows down, the mouth. Above, near the missing draw-
> string of the drawstring bag, Bea sees bits of her black
> hair reflected. She is faceted like The Fly. Vincent Price
> would recognize her. (p. 178)

If one ignores the temptation to equate an empty bag and an empty womb, one is nevertheless brought face to face with a self-described horror. A multi-role-playing creature who would be mother-daughter-artist-wife-lecturer-lover-heroine, she fails at all. The desire of the sensitive woman to do all things well is evident. She is not perfect; ergo, she describes herself as a creature from a horror film. Resembling other women in their multiplicity of roles and their diffusion of interests does not help a person to establish a separate self. In order to find Lena, she must know who Lena's mother is. In order to find herself, she must first experience a process of individuation which resembles disintegration, like shattered facets of a mirror. Bea continues on her journey.

The experience on Sea Island has promised knowledge. The shells on a dresser in this fictional den of romance correspond to Bea's collected thoughts. The narrator foreshadows other events: "She will come, in time, in two years' time, to know these shells intimately. Now time antecedes and predicts" (p. 124).

Shells emerge once again in her life in Florida. Here, where the sea pounds into pilings and leaves the shells strewn on the beach, a delicate Aphrodite would be drowned or crushed. In collecting shells along these beaches, Beatrix finds a rare gastropod that has cracked and repaired itself (p. 237), indicative of her own condition--wounded, empty, but remaining. Like the cracked shell, she too is exhibited at parties by her retired friend, "his exhibit, his seashell on driftwood" (p. 238). The drawings of her daughter, with women crying seashell tears, remind the reader of the condition of women at large, but especially of Beatrix, who has been "left, bereft" (p. 239).

Beatrix resembles the shell because she, too, has been in the watery deep and emerged with arms unoccupied, womb abandoned, exterior hardened, and interior chafed. Her descent is unplanned and unwilling. She is pulled down by her daughter; she pulls her daughter down. Elsewhere, the attempted assassination takes place daily, eternally--the narcissistic mother, the needy child; the needy artist, the selfish and demanding child. The narrator realizes: "To comfort someone else is to discomfort one's self. Which is what Beatrix was not willing to do" (p. 111), at least not until she has a fortune and can bestow love and attention without being deprived herself. And so, the fight alienates the two women. The narrator claims: "Beatrix destroyed the present, but, much worse, the past. Did the sea surface with her to crack her against these pilings, shuck her, leave her with other empty shells of people?" (pp. 240-41). Failing in motherhood, which is by all traditional accounts woman's most important and fulfilling role, Beatrix "will lock firmly the luggage of her life, her typewriter, suitcase, cosmetic bag, and record nothing, accomplish no distance, alter no tired appearance" (p. 241).

Beatrix's journey to the interior and to the past has brought her to the realization of the importance of mothering. A failure there pales successes elsewhere. To hurt one's daughter is to hurt not only the child one has, but also the child one was, the child one is, and the child one wants to be. No matter how fierce and triumphant the dragon-slayer, if the dragon is one's mother, one's daughter, or both in one-

169

self, victory is hollow. To be more than an empty survivor, to have an acceptable self-image, Beatrix must rely on Lena's final generosity. When the daughter returns, the artist and the woman within are united. The narrator can then report women conducting their own lives, singing and dancing because they are unafraid. Beatrix's journey to the interior highlights the interdependence of mother and child and the importance of an integrated self-image.


## LADY ORACLE

In another modern journey to the interior, *Lady Oracle* (1976), Margaret Atwood presents the multiple fantasies of the heroine and, in so doing, raises questions about the nature of myth-making and the process of self-deception. The novel begins with the death of the narrator; not until later does the reader learn that her drowning was staged and her rebirth one in a series.

As a young girl, Joan Foster had seen her ambitions stifled. Her mother had asked her to renounce the wings she was supposed to wear in the "Butterfly Frolic" ballet because, being fat, Joan was "more like a giant caterpillar than a butterfly, more like a white grub" (p. 47). But, as the narrator confesses, "The wings were what I really longed for" (p. 45) and "I was hoping for magic transformations even then" (p. 46).

She tries to construct her own family romance, to mythicize the birth of herself as heroine, but she has so little self-esteem that she can only ask herself, "What could have persuaded my mother to take me in if she hadn't been obliged to?" (p. 89). Her question suggests that the self-abasement of women is so strong that they cannot create an effective myth of the heroine. They can only fantasize about the artist as heroine, as Joan proceeds to do. She recalls having seen the Fat Lady at a fairground, though she can't recall whether the harem girls were in the same tent. The two mesh in her mind as freaks, monsters, circus grotesques--females on display to please men or to please an audience.

When her aunt dies, leaving a legacy provided that she lose a hundred pounds, Joan disciplines herself and becomes different, a thin person, born fully-grown. She starts her new life in England as Louisa

Delacourt, hides her past, loses her virginity, begins writing historical romances, flies back to North America when her mother dies, marries, and begins another life there as Arthur's wife.

When her husband sees pictures of her old self, "her face puffed and empty as a mongoloid idiot's" (p. 91), she evades the truth:

> *Instead, I retreated behind the camouflage of myself as Arthur perceived me. . . . He wanted me to be inept and vulnerable, it's true, but only superficially. Underneath this was another myth: that I could permit myself to be inept and vulnerable only because I had a core of strength, a reservoir of support and warmth that could be drawn on when needed.*
>
> *Every myth is a version of the truth, and the warmth and support were there all right. I learned commiseration early . . . (p. 92)*

The clenched teeth of the thin, svelte, stylish harem-girl stifle the Fat Lady's expression of her desire to fly, her hope for fame, and her need for approval. While watching television with Arthur, she fantasizes about the Fat Lady on a high wire carrying a tiny umbrella, a prop the narrator explains: "This was a substitute for the wings which I longed to pin on her. Even in my fantasies I remained faithful to a few ground rules of reality" (p. 102). The performing Fat Lady (the natural Earth Mother who is trying to become the independent female artist) is not a likely candidate for wings.

Living her multiple life as wife, scullery-maid, secret gothic-romance writer, and grub for the publication of a radical group founded by her husband, she retraces her journey. She realizes that "for Arthur there were true paths, several of them perhaps, but only one at a time. For me there were no paths at all. Thickets, ditches, ponds, labyrinths, morasses, but no paths" (p. 170). There may have been as many Arthurs as Joans, but the narrator claims, "The difference was that I was simultaneous, whereas Arthur was a sequence" (p. 211).

While married and secretly writing her gothic romances--a genre much deplored by the philosophizing, political crowd she had married into--

171

she also explores automatic writing before her candle-lit mirror, enters therein a "dark, shining corridor," and frequently explores its mysteries:

> *There was the sense of going along a narrow passage*
> *led downward, the certainty that if I could only turn the*
> *next corner or the next--for these journeys became*
> *longer--I would find the thing, the truth or word or*
> *person that was mine, that was waiting for me. (p. 221)*

From these sessions, she collects words and phrases and turns them into poems with a heroine who "lived under the earth somewhere, or inside something, a cave or a huge building, sometimes she was on a boat. She was enormously powerful, almost like a goddess, but it was an unhappy power" (p. 222). She collects the poems in a book and becomes famous. Her life opens into other fantasy-worlds, including that of a bizarre lover, The Royal Porcupine. But when the lover turns possessive, sports a crew-cut and T-shirt, and wants an ordinary marriage, she is disenchanted and guilt-ridden. As an artist who rejects conventional patterns of life, she desponds: "I felt like a monster, a large, blundering monster, irredeemably shallow" (p. 271). The Fat Lady skates on thin ice in her fantasies (p. 273).

Because her ex-lover is threatening to kill her and because she is wanted for a bombing, instigated by her husband's radical political group and harmlessly carried out by her, she devises a fake drowning and flies to Italy. Her life is viewed in retrospect while she finishes her manuscript of *Charlotte at Redmond Grange.* This gothic romance reflects the circumstances of Joan's life, allows her to examine aspects of that life, provides a means for Joan to escape a more painful examination of her personality, and lets her fantasize about alternative outcomes. Stuck in Italy without funds or friends, she realizes that both her fantasies and her chosen lifestyles turn into traps. She labels herself an artist, an escape artist who enjoys extricating herself from dangerous situations. She plans another escape, swearing that she will henceforth dance for no one but herself.

Pretending to dance, whirling across the room, she imagines wings growing from her shoulders and an arm encircling her; suddenly she dances over broken glass and seriously cuts her feet. She remembers the *Red Shoes* ballet:

172

*You could dance, or you could have the love of a good*
*man. But you were afraid to dance, because you had*
*this unnatural fear that if you danced they'd cut your*
*feet off . . . . Finally you overcame your fear and*
*danced, and they cut your feet off. The good man went*
*away too, because you wanted to dance. (p. 335)*

She denigrates herself, becomes paranoid about what the neighbors
think of her, and imagines that they believe her to be a female monster.
She drafts her final chapter with several outcomes, depending on her
fears and problems of the moment. Finally Lady Redmond, the fifth,
enters the maze and finds four women in the central plot, all claiming to
be Lady Redmond, including a fat lady wearing a pair of pink tights and
false wings pinned to her back. Felicia Redmond protests that she is
Lady Redmond, but they assure her: " *'Every man has more than one*
*wife. Sometimes all at once, sometimes one at a time, sometimes ones*
*he doesn't even know about'* " (p. 341). The way back is overgrown,
and she is trapped. The escape door is blocked by a seductive young
man who transforms himself: *"The flesh fell away from his face,*
*revealing the skull behind it"* (p. 343). A knock at her hotel door stops
Joan from proceeding further on her manuscript. Frightened, she
opens the door and hits the person on the other side with a Cinzano
bottle. Obviously, she feels disintegrated when called upon to be
several women at once, especially while role-playing for her husband.
The artist in Joan envisions him or men in general as death. In addition,
her precarious position--as artist/woman--on the tightrope of society
makes her paranoid.

Realizing that she has hit a stranger, Joan unsnarls some of the con-
fusing strands of her life, nurses the stitched and bandaged intruder,
and prepares to fall in love with him, having begun to feel that he
knows the real her. As Joan says, ''Maybe because I've never hit anyone else with a bottle, so they never got to see that part of me. Neither
did I, come to think of it'' (p. 345).

She has learned to release the destructive force prompted by the face
submerged at the bottom of the corridor, peering from the window of a
tower, searching from the prow of a boat, and staring from the center of
the maze. Since the muse seems to be Joan's mother, Atwood implies
that some of this female artist's explosive frustration stems from her

173

conflict in establishing a sexual or positional identity separate from her mother's. Fantasy allows the artist to imagine an escape from the labyrinth of heterosexual relations and from the sorrows attached to her sexual identity. But fantasy can effect only a temporary release.

In a pastiche of myths that parody gothic novels, modern and hospital romances, incomprehensible poetry with mythic overtones, and the daily newspapers, Margaret Atwood has created a comic journey into the creation of a novel and the interior of an artist's mind, with just enough grim truth in all the humor to make the reader smile through clenched teeth. These myths of the captive Earth Mother, of woman as victim, as muse, and as monster are seductive. A woman can see aspects of herself mirrored there, feel caged by the myths, and want to escape. But, if to escape one has to be Dumbo the Elephant, chances of flying are limited and the suggested self-image is ridiculous. Furthermore, hitting a man on the head and then nursing him back from a weakened to a healthy condition is not auspicious as a new beginning. Comically, it smacks of the hospital romance. Seriously, the heroine's escape provides a grim outlook of eternal power plays when release is managed at the expense of a man's health, stature, and psyche.

The importance of this journey to the interior lies in its use of mythic tradition, its emphasis on the suggestiveness of myths to women, and its indication of the numerous ways in which these myths can be interpreted and manipulated. The novel implies that women *can* lead assertive and exciting lives. To fantasize about such excitement in traditional modes, however, is to steer oneself into a trap. Dreaming of the romantic hero leads one to the center of the maze, where death awaits.

To escape the morass of sexual fantasies based on patriarchal myths, the artist must have an imagination, a sense of humor, an understanding of her vulnerability, and a readiness for the next entrapment. By poking fun at the Fat Lady and laughing at the harem girl, Margaret Atwood temporarily escapes the snares awaiting the artist/woman who needs approval.

# SUMMARY

Looking back on these journeys to the interior, one sees certain images and themes recur: images of isolation (including the artist's room of her own), of entrapment, of flight, and of rebirth.

The most prevalent theme is alienation from society, conveyed by images of self-imposed solitude or flight from restraint. The "secret self" of Mary Olivier, the "second self" of Thea Kronborg, and the "beloved hated secret self" of Miriam Henderson all suggest the divisiveness of such alienation. This theme is long-standing in the novels of the artist. As Maurice Beebe declares:

> The main characteristics of the artist are unchanged
> from the first artist-novels to those of our own time.
> Among those characteristics . . . is that ability to look
> on at the self from a distance which separates the man
> who acts from the man who observes and sets up a
> conflict between the urge to "live" and the temptation
> to seek solitude. [22]

But this theme of the split self emerges somewhat differently in the novels written by and about women. Diane Filby Gillespie believes the cause lies in sexual stereotyping: "Because [men] do not confront a tradition that insists upon their incapacity in any field other than intimate human relationships, their conflict is of a different nature." [23] Whereas the man feels split between personal and social being, the woman experiences that split and the separation of sexual and personal identity. The language and imagery in these journeys reflect that distinct division. For instance, when Esther Greenwood, in *The Bell Jar,* despairs over her isolation from society, she does not say, "Why was I so apart?" She says, "Why was I so unmaternal and apart?" (p. 182) because she sees maternity as her biological destiny, at least insofar as that destiny is presently defined by society. Although both male and female artists often want to escape the restrictions of social convention, women face the confinement of their sexual identity as well.

Novelists of both sexes use images to suggest restraint, such as the nets confining Dedalus to Ireland. But the female artist has a particular affinity for images of imprisoning glass--the bell jar, the bottle, the glass vase, or the spun-glass illusion. Since women traditionally depend on others for support and long for approval as an assurance of sexual identity, the image they project to society is of paramount importance. They live in glass houses. The artists who break out crash against the pane or cut themselves on the glass, destroying their artistic dexterity. Those who don't escape suffocate under the bell jar.

Because they are repeatedly told, "Women can't paint, can't write," female artists making their journey to the interior choke out this evident theme of suffocation. Their *Künstlerromanen* are gasps, pleas for air. The enigmatic sphinx remains mute; its artist feels suffocated. The mythic Earth Mother in *Surfacing* thinks that "her neck must have closed over" (p. 106) and destroys her paints. The pilgrim-writer fears suffocation in the temple of adoration. The singer's throat freezes at home, where she is expected to be conciliatory. In the stifling air of her home, the pianist's hands cramp. The hero-ine's pen leaks or clogs, depending on the air space society allows. Longing for release from this suffocation, these artists dream of freedom.

Flight, as an escape from society's confinement, is an evident theme and wings a familiar image for the over-achiever, as Maurice Shroder suggests by the title of his critical survey, *Icarus: The Image of the Artist in French Romanticism.* However, Shroder also unwittingly indicates the particular problem of the female artist working within that tradition when he explains Mme. de Staël's dramatization of the different modes of the artist in *Corinne* as "a reversal of the sexes." [24] Because this polarity between woman and artist persists, the flight imagery in their journeys is distinctive. The means of flight receive special emphases. Jong describes Isadora's wings as "borrowed" and attaches her heroine to a husband named "Wing." In *Lady Oracle* Atwood describes her heroine's wings as ludicrous attachments to an Earth Mother figure or as skimpy wings on a Fat Lady. For the heroines of Richardson, Sinclair, and Lessing, flying is possible only in a dream or a trance, and the return necessitates a death-in-life of woman or artist.

Birds are frequent and obvious images in novels of the artist. In *The Flight of the Gander,* Campbell claims, "The bird of the shaman is one of particular character and power, endowing him with an ability to fly in trance beyond all bounds of life, and yet return."[25] The gander is male. The goose has more than a little trouble flying out of range of the hunter. Safe return is not guaranteed.

In *Künstlerromanen* written by and about women, birds are broken, crippled, strangled, or hung. In *The Song of the Lark,* the eagle is contrasted with small nesting birds. The heroine's artistic self consumes the girl she was (p. 500), just as the eagle devours smaller birds. In *Surfacing* hunters willfully mangle a heron and hang it upside down from a tree (p. 115). The title of *The Story of Avis* hints at the attempted flight of its heroine. In this novel, birds crash against the lighthouse window during storms and wash up along the shore. The image reflects the life story of the main character, named "Avis" to highlight the analogy. The male protagonist in *Orlando* flies; the female artist is confined to fantasy, unable to net the goose of winged imagination.

Whereas dancing to one's own real or imagined tune as an image of independence is not the sole province of women, in their *Künstler-romanen* the image is bizarre. Dancing with male partners, they are often swept indecorously off their feet, tossed to the ground, or paired with death. Without partners, they run the risk of cutting, mangling, or infecting their feet so that they can hardly stand alone, not to mention dance. Indeed, the feet and legs of female artists receive inordinate attention. Natalie Petesch's heroine draws the mother in a family portrait with "her legs truncated" (p. 215) and even speaks of gnawing off her own foot in order to "free herself from the love trap" (p. 215).

If she cannot fly, dance, or walk away, and cannot bear to remain invisible, the artist must change. A woman who wants to voice her feelings and declare her presence must create herself anew, just as the male artist has recreated himself in the myth of the birth of the hero. Unfortunately, when the female artist tries during her journey to the interior to create the myth of the artist as heroine, she usually miscarries, aborts, or gives birth to a monster. It is this particular imagery which is so striking in the female voyage to the interior. Like the male artist, she journeys to caves, wells, pools, lakes, oceans, oxygen tents, quarries, lonely rooms, and baths in order to give birth. But the female artist's well is often dry; the quarry must be violently blasted before it will hold water; and rebirth from the womb of cave, earth, or pool often

177

strips her womanhood or damages her mirror-image (like Esther Greenwood's reflection, neither man nor woman).

Most intriguing in the imagery of these journeys is the frequent mention of the labyrinth or maze, where the heroine faces dissolution or confronts her demon of destruction. Whereas the typical mythic hero destroys the minotaur, marries the heroine, and assumes the throne, the heroine must accept the demon, reject the hero, and live in misery if she is to retain her identity as an artist. Such an artistic rebirth involves the creation of a freak, a monster, a dybbuk, or a Medusa.

Having discovered this tendency of the female artist to create or to label herself a monster, I applaud Ellen Moers's sensitive reading of Mary Shelley's *Frankenstein* and her statement about the artistic creation of females: "To give *visual* form to the fear of self, to hold anxiety up to the Gothic mirror of the imagination, may well be more common in the writings of women than of men."[26]

Despite attempts in their journeys inward to create self-images divorced from the patriarchal perspective, as inheritors of its myths, female artists continue to fall victim to society's buffeting, to create the female dragon, or to abort the self in one form or another. Nevertheless, an important aspect of their inner journey is its focus on the new *mythos:* a myth of the birth of the artist as heroine and a recognition of this offspring, no matter how ugly or weak.

## Chapter V

## CONCLUSION: A BEGINNING

*"Cultivation precedes fruition."* [1]
--Cynthia Ozick

The literary woman inherits an obvious tradition of myths, including those of the artist (like Faust) and of Demeter/Persephone. Acting simultaneously as woman, artist, and inheritor of that tradition, she plays roles therein defined as mutually exclusive. These patriarchal myths, her own family relationships, and an ambivalent self-image unite to mold or to mute her creation of the artist as heroine.

The distinct separations of this study are not present in the life of the real or fictional artist-heroine; the occasional overlapping of ideas in these chapters reflects a simultaneity she experiences. Myths and her womanly role interact; the figure of Faust's Eternal Woman blurs and becomes Persephone or Demeter. Her perception of self as one or all of these mythic heroines sometimes slows individuation, and her journey to the interior, as a woman, often brings her back to the Terrible/Good Mother she wants to be and to escape. With a woman's body, the artist-heroine is continually reminded of her war against social constructs that restrict her as an artist; yet that war plays havoc with her self-image. Forging a new self in the midst of those iron-clad restrictions, the heroine identifies, as an artist, with the lame and deformed Hepaestus.

The distinctive images and the structure of her mythic journey reflect her struggle. Whereas the hero's mythic return heralds salvation, the heroine's return involves recognition of herself as female in a society that denigrates the serious artistry of women. That recognition promotes a rejection of herself as woman, an acceptance of herself as monster, or a welcoming of death-in-life as preferable to the struggle.

Looking back on these novels and the pattern of their journeys, one can see that the novel of the artist as heroine has many functions. It justifies the artist's lonely existence, explains her failure (as artist or as woman), exhibits her ambivalence, pleads for the approval of her mother or daughter, insists on the need for alternatives to current stifling conditions, or laughs "a little too loud" at her own contortions as she strives to escape. The only treasure or talisman won during the journey is the novel that records it, often a storehouse against future depression.

None of these novels depicts a self-made, fully integrated human being, artist and woman. Recent novels focus on the courage necessary for the development of an independent, creative artist. Some novelists insist that women must acknowledge their own capabilities and stop acting like victims, even though they may continue to be victimized. Several suggest that the artist may soon be able to create the new *mythos* necessary to depict the integration of a female who is both courageous and womanly. The task is left to future mothers and daughters.

Such a *mythos* cannot spring from the head of women who, though wise, have only a patriarchal heritage of myths that seduce them into playing other roles. The artist as heroine believes that she can create art or feels compelled to try; she would like to do so without sacrificing her womanhood and without feeling guilty. Each novelist studied here insists on her heroine's natural right as an artist. Together, these writers cultivate ground previously seeded; their efforts will foster the growth of a new *mythos*, a new base for the female artist.

This study also cultivates that growth by identifying distinctive mythic patterns and images in the works written by and about female artists. However, this work prompts as many questions as it answers.

For instance, several psychologists and sociologists believe that myths may determine how we dream or fantasize. Like Susan Brownmiller, I believe that fairy tales and legends affect the psyche of the young girl. In what way do existing myths pattern our lives? Now that more feminist psychologists and psychiatrists are in the field, perhaps their analyses will generate a *Birth of the Artist as Heroine* in the same way that Otto Rank's analyses fostered *The Birth of the Artist as Hero*. Whether or not such a study evolves, the question of what effect myth has on individuals generally and on writers particularly needs further research.

Despite touching upon possible psychological bases of myth, this study pretends to be neither psychoanalytic nor biographical criticism that would explore the individual novelist's attempt to give birth to herself in the *Künstlerroman*. The study does suggest that, in the hands of experts, such biographical or psychoanalytic explorations might prove profitable.

In addition to asking psychological questions that may be conundrums, this study raises questions concerning the history of the novel of the artist as heroine. As previously mentioned, Beebe claims that the essential elements of artist-novels remain constant from age to age, whereas Gerald Jay Goldberg claims that essential differences exist, depending on the era. I have focused on the similarity of structural patterns and images found in the novels of the artist as heroine. Now what is needed is an historical approach that notes variations, details the effect of time or events on these patterns, and shows trends, if there are any. Looking at the dates of the novels examined, for instance, I see that they are clustered in groups--at the turn of the century, in the thirteen years from 1915 to 1928, and in the last fourteen years, 1962-1976. Why is there a void in the 1940's? the 1950's? Do events help or hinder the germination of the novel of the artist as heroine? What is the relationship between events and style or characterization? Linda Pannill focused on this relationship in her dissertation, "The Artist-Heroine in American Fiction, 1890-1920." [2] But a broad perspective is necessary in order to identify individual talent as it emerges in the tradition of the novel of the artist as heroine. The Euhemerist might profitably combine mythological and historical methodologies to investigate the relationship between history and the emergence of a myth of the artist as heroine.

In order to research from such an historical perspective, as well as from others, the scholar needs the textual archaelogists to precede her. Some novels of the artist, such as Mona Caird's *The Daughters of*

*Danaus* (1894) and Frances Brooke's *Excursion* (1777), are so rare that libraries will not circulate them. These and other rare books and manuscripts (still to be unearthed) need to be made accessible to scholars. One of the novels in this study, *The Story of Avis,* is newly issued in a series of *Rediscovered Fiction by American Woman.* Additional digging is needed to develop a more complete picture of the artist-heroine and to trace her mythic journey.

I do not wish by these suggestions to foster a separatist movement. *Künstlerromanen* written by and about women are a part of the mainstream and have influenced its direction. That influence also deserves further investigation. However, both this study and the *mythos* that describes the conflict of the artist as heroine grow from the realization that, at present, such insights seem obvious only from a woman's perspective.

# NOTES

## Chapter I

1 Joseph Campbell, "Bios and Mythos: Prolegomena to a Science of Mythology," in *Psychoanalysis and Culture: Essays in Honor of Géza Róheim*, ed. George B. Wilbur and Warner Muensterberger (New York: International Universities Press, 1951), p. 342.

2 Claude Lévi-Strauss, "The Structural Study of Myth," in *Myth: A Symposium*, ed. Thomas A. Sebeok (Philadelphia: American Folklore Society, 1955), p. 53.

3 Ibid., p. 62.

4 Ibid., p. 52.

5 Bronislaw Malinowski, *Myth in Primitive Psychology* (New York: W.W. Norton, 1926), p. 19.

6 Joseph Campbell, *The Flight of the Wild Gander: Explorations in the Mythological Dimension* (New York: Viking Press, 1969), p. 19.

7 Ibid., p. 118.

8 Elizabeth Janeway, *Man's World, Woman's Place: A Study in Social Mythology* (New York: Wm. Morrow, 1971), p. 26.

9 Ibid., p. 13.

10 Wallace Douglas, "The Meaning of 'Myth' in Modern Criticism," *Modern Philology*, 50 (1953), 232.

11 Alan W. Watts, *Myth and Ritual in Christianity* (London: Thomas, 1954), p. 7. My preference for this definition reveals my pluralistic bias.

12 Campbell, *Flight*, p. 75.

13 Otto Rank, "The Myth of the Birth of the Hero: A Psychological Interpretation of Mythology," trans. F. Robbins and Smith Ely Jelliffe, in *The Myth of the Birth of the Hero and Other Writings* (1914; rpt.

New York: Vintage Books, 1964), p. 11, Rank argues: "Investigators who apply an exclusively 'natural' scheme of interpretations have been unable, in any sense--in their endeavor to discover the original sense of the myths--to get away entirely from a psychological process such as must be assumed similarly for the creators of the myths."

[14] Philip Wheelwright, "Notes on Mythopoeia," *Sewanee Review,* 59 (1951), 583-84.

[15] Northrop Frye, *Anatomy of Criticism: Four Essays* (Princeton: Princeton University Press, 1957), p. 325. He is describing the "parabolic dramatic structure" of the Bible.

[16] Rank, p. 65.

[17] Ibid., p. 85.

[18] Carl G. Jung, *"Wandlungen und Symbole der Libido,"* *Jahrbuch für Psychoanalyse,* 5 (1912), 356; as quoted by Rank, pp. 85-86.

[19] Frye, *Anatomy,* p. 17.

[20] Philip Wheelwright, "The Semantic Approach to Myth," *Myth: A Symposium,* p. 96.

[21] Ernst Kris, *Psychoanalytic Explorations in Art* (New York: International Universities Press, Inc., 1952), p. 83.

[22] Erich Heller, *The Artist's Journey into the Interior and Other Essays* (New York: Random House, 1965), p. 86.

[23] Ibid., p. 195.

[24] Gerald Jay Goldberg, "The Artist-Novel in Transition," *English Fiction in Transition,* 4 (1961), 25.

[25] Frye, "The Archetypes of Literature," *Kenyon Review,* 13 (1951), 107.

[26] Joseph Campbell, *The Hero with a Thousand Faces,* 2nd ed. (Princeton: Princeton University Press, 1968), p. 35.

[27] Ibid.

[28] Ralph Linton, *The Cultural Background of Personality* (New York: Appleton-Crofts, Inc., 1945), p. 129.

[29] Kris, p. 65.

[30] Maurice Beebe, *Ivory Towers and Sacred Founts: The Artist as Hero in Fiction from Goethe to Joyce* (New York: New York University Press, 1964), p. 71.

[31] Ibid., p. 77.

# NOTES

## Chapter II

1 Johann Wolfgang von Goethe, *Faust: A Tragedy*, trans. Walter Arndt, ed. Cyrus Hamlin (New York: W.W. Norton, 1976), p. 308.

2 Erica Jong, "Writer who 'flew' to sexy fame talks about being a woman," *Vogue* (March 1977), p. 158.

3 Faust, p. 27.

4 Beebe, p. 13.

5 Hans Eichner, "The Eternal Feminine: An Aspect of Goethe's Ethics," *Transactions of the Royal Society of Canada*, IV, 9 (1971), 235-44; rpt. in *Faust*, p. 624.

6 *Faust*, p. 8.

7 Eichner, p. 624.

8 Judd Marmor, "Changing Patterns of Femininity," in *The Marriage Relationship*, ed. Salo Rosenbaum and Ian Alger (New York: Basic Books, 1968); rpt. in *Psychoanalysis and Women: Contributions to New Theory and Therapy*, ed. Jean Baker Miller, M.D. (New York: Brunner/Mazel, 1973), p. 200.

9 Leon Salzman, "Psychology of the Female: A New Look," *Archives of General Psychiatry*, 17 (August 1967), 195-203; rpt. in *Psychoanalysis and Women*, p. 184.

10 Nancy Chodorow, "Family Structure and Feminine Personality," in *Woman, Culture, and Society*, ed. Michelle Zimbalist Rosaldo and Louise Lamphere (Stanford, Calif.: Stanford University Press, 1974), p. 55.

11 Nancy Chodorow, "Being and Doing: A Cross-Culture Examination of the Socialization of Males and Females," in *Woman in Sexist Society: Studies in Power and Powerlessness*, ed. Vivian Gornick and Barbara K. Moran (New York and London: Basic Books, 1971), p. 184.

[12] Mary Ellmann, *Thinking about Women* (New York: Harcourt, Brace & World, 1968), p. 64.

[13] Arnold C. Bergstraesser, "The Nature of Man," in *Goethe's Image of Man and Society* (Chicago: Henry Regnery, 1949); rpt. in *Goethe's Faust Part One: Essays in Criticism,* ed. John B. Vickery and J'nan Sellery (Belmont, Calif.: Wadsworth, 1969), p. 148.

[14] Bergstraesser, p. 148.

[15] Sylvia Plath, *The Bell Jar* (1963; rpt. New York: Harper & Row, 1971), p. 104. Hereafter, references will be included in the text. This novel was originally published under the pseudonym Victoria Lucas.

[16] Willa Cather, *The Song of the Lark* (Boston and New York: Houghton Mifflin Company, 1943), p. vi. Hereafter, references will be included in the text.

[17] Dorothy Richardson, *Pilgrimage* (London: J.M. Dent & Sons, 1967), II, 187. References to all four volumes of this edition will hereafter be included in the text.

[18] Judith Bardwick, *Psychology of Women: A Study of Bio-Cultural Conflicts* (New York: Harper & Row, 1971), p. 158.

[19] Carol Pearson, "The Artist," *Who Am I This Time?: Female Portraits in British and American Literature,* eds. Carol Pearson and Katherine Pope (New York: McGraw Hill Book Company, 1976), p. 199.

[20] Ibid.

[21] *Faust,* p. 34.

[22] Leon Edel, "D.R., 1882-1957," *Modern Fiction Studies,* 4 (1958), 168.

[23] Virginia Woolf, *Orlando* (New York: Harcourt, Brace and Company, 1928), p. 189. References to this edition will hereafter be included in the text.

[24] Patricia Ann Meyer Spacks, *The Female Imagination* (New York: Random House, 1971), p. 170.

[25] Zelda Fitzgerald, *Save Me the Waltz* (1932; rpt. Carbondale and Edwardsville: Southern Illinois Press, 1967), p. 37. Hereafter, references will be included in the text.

[26] Natalie Petesch, *The Odyssey of Katinou Kalokovich* (Tampa, Fla.: United Sisters, 1974), p. 16. Hereafter, references will be included in the text.

[27] Muriel Spark, *The Public Image* (London: MacMillan, 1968), p. 52.

[28] Doris Lessing, *The Golden Notebook* (New York: Simon and Schuster, 1962), p. 502. Hereafter, references will be included in the text.

29 Ellen Peck Killoh, "The Woman Writer and the Element of Destruction," *College English*, 34 (October 1972), 31.

# NOTES

## Chapter III

[1] Phyllis Chesler, *Women and Madness* (Garden City: Doubleday & Company, 1972), p. 302.

[2] Susan Brownmiller, *Against Our Will: Men, Women and Rape* (New York: Simon and Schuster, 1975), pp. 309, 327.

[3] Ellen Moers, *Literary Women: The Great Writers* (New York: Anchor-Doubleday, 1977), p. xiv.

[4] Virginia Woolf, *A Room of One's Own* (1929; rpt. New York: Harcourt, Brace, 1957), pp. 76-77.

[5] Chodorow, "Being and Doing," p. 184.

[6] Philip E. Slater, "Toward a Dualistic Theory of Identification," *Merrill-Palmer Quarterly of Behavior and Development*, 7, (April 1961), 113.

[7] Chodorow, "Family Structure and Feminine Personality," pp. 59, 60, 65.

[8] Chesler, p. 19. To Chesler, mothering is not restricted by biological relationships, but is dependent on *nurturance:* "The consistent and readily available gift of physical, domestic, and emotional support in childhood, together with the added gift of compassion and respect in adulthood" (fn, pp. 18-19).

[9] Bardwick, p. 139.

[10] Ibid., p. 117, fn. 2.

[11] Ibid.

[12] Chesler, p. 18.

[13] Shulamith Firestone, *The Dialectic of Sex: The Case for Feminist Revolution* (New York: Wm. Morrow, 1970), p. 147.

[14] Dorothy Dinnerstein, *The Mermaid and the Minotaur: Sexual*

*Arrangements and Human Malaise* (New York: Harper & Row, 1976), p. 85.

15 David Cooper, *The Death of the Family* (New York: Pantheon Books, 1970).

16 Erich Neumann, *The Great Mother: An Analysis of the Archetype,* trans. Ralph Manheim, Bollingen, 7 (Princeton: Princeton University Press, 2nd ed., 1963), p. 305.

17 Pearson and Pope, pp. 194-95.

18 Edith Hamilton, *Mythology: Timeless Tales of Gods and Heroes* (New York: New American Library, 1969), p. 48.

19 C. Kerényi, *Eleusis: Archetypal Image of Mother and Daughter,* trans. Ralph Manheim, Bollingen 65, 4 (New York: Pantheon Books, 1967), p. 130.

20 Ibid., p. 147.

21 Ibid., p. xxxii.

22 Ibid., p. 174.

23 Adrienne Rich, *Of Woman Born: Motherhood as Experience and Institution* (New York: W.W. Norton, 1976), p. 94.

24 Ibid., p. 224.

25 Ibid., p. 237.

26 Ibid., p. 229.

27 Wheelwright, "Notes on Mythopoeia," p. 586.

28 Robert R. Holt, "The Development of Primary Process: A Structural View," in *Motives and Thought: Psychoanalytic Essays in Honor of David Rapaport,* ed. Robert R. Holt (New York: International Universities Press, 1967), p. 375.

29 Chesler, p. 20.

30 Brownmiller, p. 333.

31 Chesler, p. 29.

32 May Sinclair, *Mary Olivier: A Life* (New York: The Macmillan Company, 1919), p. 4. Hereafter, page references will be indicated in the text.

33 Rich, p. 34.

34 Chodorow, "Family Structure and Feminine Personality," pp. 64-65.

35 Karen Horney, "The Flight from Womanhood," *International Journal of Psycho-Analysis*, 7, (1926), 324-29; rpt. in *Psychoanalysis and Women*, p. 13.

36 Alfred Adler, "Sex," in *Understanding Human Nature*, trans. W. Béran Wolfe (1927; rpt. Greenwich, Conn.: Fawcett, 1954),

pp. 102-22; rpt. in *Psychoanalysis and Women,* p. 36.

37 Rich, p. 253.

38 Ibid., p. 243.

39 Mary Austin, *A Woman of Genius* (Garden City: Doubleday, Page, 1912), pp. 19-20. Hereafter, references will be indicated in the text.

40 Robert Seidenberg, "Is Anatomy Destiny?" in *Marriage in Life and Literature* (New York: Philosophical Library, 1970), p. 142.

41 Pamela Hansford Johnson, *Catherine Carter* (London: Macmillan and Co., Ltd., 1968), p. 219. Hereafter, page references will be indicated in the text.

42 Bardwich, p. 59.

43 Rich, p. 252.

44 Joseph L. Blotner, "Mythical Patterns in *To the Lighthouse,*" *PMLA,* 71 (1956), 552.

45 Virginia Woolf, *To the Lighthouse* (1927; rpt. New York: Harcourt, Brace & Company, 1955), p. 13. Hereafter, page references will be indicated in the text.

46 Sharon Wood Proudfit, "Lily Briscoe's Painting: A Key to Personal Relations in *To the Lighthouse,*" *Criticism,* 13 (Winter 1971), 26-39. She argues that Lily 1) slays the ghost of her attraction to Mrs. Ramsey and 2) acknowledges that Mr. Ramsay also reaches a right relationship with his deceased wife (p. 38). Herbert Marder, *Feminism and Art: Study of Virginia Woolf* (Chicago: University of Chicago Press, 1968), p. 57, argues that the painting is an expression of harmony.

47 Marder, p. 125, claims, "Virginia Woolf saw the universe as the scene of an eternal conflict between opposites, corresponding . . . to masculine and feminine principles." But he calls Virginia Woolf's mind androgynous and the picture a harmony which Mrs. Ramsay has been able to afford Lily.

48 Elizabeth Stuart Phelps [Ward], *The Story of Avis* (1879; rpt. New York: Arno Press, 1977), p. 201. Hereafter, page references will be indicated in the text.

49 Erica Jong, *Fear of Flying* (New York: Holt, Rinehart and Winston, 1973), p. 42. Hereafter, page references will be indicated in the text.

50 Chesler, p. 30.

51 Ovid, *Metamorphoses,* trans. Rolfe Humphries (Bloomington: Indiana University Press, 1961), p. 124.

52 Ibid., p. 123.

53 Margaret Atwood, *Lady Oracle* (New York: Simon and Schuster, 1976), p. 213. Hereafter, page references will be indicated in the text.

54 Margaret Atwood, *Surfacing* (Toronto: McClelland and Stewart, Limited, 1972), p. 52. Hereafter, page references will be indicated in the text.

55 May Sarton, *Mrs. Stevens Hears the Mermaids Singing* (New York: W.W. Norton, 1965), p. 18. Hereafter, page references will be indicated in the text.

56 E.M. Broner, *Her Mothers* (New York: Holt, Rinehart and Winston, 1975), p. 74. Hereafter, page references will be indicated in the text.

57 Rich, p. 253.

58 Ibid., p. 247.

# NOTES

## Chapter IV

[1] Woolf, *A Room of One's Own*, p. 59.

[2] Richardson, IV, 168.

[3] Anaïs Nin, "On Feminism and Creation," *Michigan Quarterly Review*, 13 (1974), 7.

[4] Mabel Blake Cohen, "Personal Identity and Sexual Identity," *Psychiatry*, 29 (1966), 3.

[5] Fred Weinstein and Gerald M. Platt, *Psychoanalytic Sociology: An Essay on the Interpretation of Historical Data and the Phenomena of Collective Behavior* (Baltimore and London: The Johns Hopkins University Press, 1973), p. 109.

[6] Rollo May, "The Daimonic in Psychotherapy," in *Love and Will* (New York: W.W. Norton, 1969), p. 133.

[7] Ibid., p. 134.

[8] Neumann, pp. 292-93.

[9] Campbell, *The Hero*, p. 35.

[10] Janeway, p. 87.

[11] Cohen, p. 4.

[12] Woolf, *A Room of One's Own*, p. 179.

[13] Horney, p. 8.

[14] Ibid., p. 5.

[15] Cohen, p. 3.

[16] Chesler, p. 18.

[17] Michelle Zimbalist Rosaldo, "Woman, Culture, and Society: A Theoretical Overview," in *Woman, Culture, and Society*, pp. 27-28.

[18] Bardwick, p. 69.

[19] Chodorow, "Family Structure and Feminine Personality," p. 59.

20 Ellmann, p. 177.

21 Ibid., p. 148.

22 Beebe, p. 65.

23 Diane Filby Gillespie, "Female Artists as Characters and Creators: The Dual Concern with Feminine Role and Feminine Fiction in the Work of May Sinclair, Dorothy Richardson, and Virginia Woolf," Diss. Univ. of Alberta 1974, p. 47. This study includes an excellent annotated bibliography of primary works featuring female artists as characters.

24 Maurice Z. Shroder, *Icarus: The Image of the Artist in French Romanticism* (Cambridge: Harvard University Press, 1969), p. 39.

25 Campbell, *Flight*, p. 167.

26 Moers, p. 163.

# NOTES

## Chapter V

[1] Cynthia Ozick, ''Women and Creativity: The Demise of the Dancing Dog,'' *Woman in Sexist Society,* p. 319.

[2] Linda Pannill, ''The Artist-Heroine in American Fiction, 1890-1920,'' Diss. Univ. of N.C., Chapel Hill, 1975.

# BIBLIOGRAPHY

## Primary Sources

Atwood, Margaret. *Lady Oracle.* New York: Simon and Schuster, 1976.
_____. *Surfacing.* Toronto: McClelland and Stewart Limited, 1972.

Austin, Mary. *A Woman of Genius.* Garden City, N.Y.: Doubleday, Page & Company, 1912.

Broner, E.M. *Her Mothers.* New York: Holt, Rinehart and Winston, 1975.

Cather, Willa. *The Song of the Lark.* Boston and New York: Houghton Mifflin Company, 1915.

Fitzgerald, Zelda. *Save Me the Waltz.* New York: Scribner, 1932; rpt. Carbondale and Edwardsville: Southern Illinois Press, 1967.

Goethe, Johann Wolfgang von. *Faust: A Tragedy.* Trans. Walter Arndt. Ed. Cyrus Hamlin. New York: W.W. Norton, 1976.

Johnson, Pamela Hansford. *Catherine Carter.* London: Macmillan, 1968; rpt. 1970.

Jong, Erica. *Fear of Flying.* New York: Holt, Rinehart and Winston, 1973.

Lessing, Doris. *The Golden Notebook.* New York: Simon and Schuster, 1962.

Ovid. *Metamorphoses.* Trans. Rolfe Humphries. Bloomington: Indiana University Press, 1961.

Petesch, Natalie L.M. *The Odyssey of Katinou Kalokovich.* Tampa, Fla.: United Sisters, 1974.

Plath, Sylvia. *The Bell Jar.* 1963; rpt. New York: Harper & Row, 1971.

Richardson, Dorothy M. *Pilgrimage.* 4 vols. London: J.M. Dent & Sons, 1967.

Sarton, May. *Mrs. Stevens Hears the Mermaids Singing*. New York: W.W. Norton, 1965.

Sinclair, May. *Mary Olivier: A Life*. New York: The Macmillan Company, 1919.

Spark, Muriel. *The Public Image*. London: Macmillan, 1968.

[Ward], Elizabeth Stuart Phelps. *The Story of Avis*. Boston: Houghton, Osgood Company, 1879; rpt. New York: Arno Press, 1977. (Rediscovered Fiction by American Women: A Personal Selection. Ed. Elizabeth Hardwick.)

Woolf, Virginia. *Orlando*. New York: Harcourt and Brace Company, 1928.

——————. *To the Lighthouse*. 1927; rpt. New York: Harcourt, Brace & Company, 1955.

## Secondary Sources

Adler, Alfred. "Sex." In *Understanding Human Nature*. Trans. W. Béran Wolfe. 1927; rpt. Greenwich, Conn.: Fawcett, 1954, pp. 102-22. Rpt. in *Psychoanalysis and Women: Contributions to New Theory and Therapy*. New York: Brunner/Mazel, 1973, pp. 33-42.

Bardwick, Judith M. *Psychology of Women: A Study of Bio-Cultural Conflicts*. New York: Harper & Row, 1971.

Beebe, Maurice. *Ivory Towers and Sacred Founts: The Artist as Hero in Fiction from Goethe to Joyce*. New York: New York University Press, 1964.

Bergstraesser, Arnold C. "The Nature of Man." In *Goethe's Image of Man and Society*. Chicago: Henry Regnery, 1949. Rpt. in *Goethe's Faust Part One: Essays in Criticism*. Ed. John B. Vickery and J'nan Sellery. Belmont, Calif.: Wadsworth, 1969, pp. 143-50.

Blotner, Joseph L. "Mythic Patterns in *To the Lighthouse*." *PMLA*, 71 (1956), 547-62.

Brownmiller, Susan. *Against Our Will: Men, Women and Rape*. New York: Simon and Schuster, 1975.

Campbell, Joseph. "Bios and Mythos: Prolegomena to a Science of Mythology." In *Psychoanalysis and Culture: Essays in Honor of Géza Róheim*. Ed. George B. Wilbur and Warner Muensterberger. New York: International Universities Press, 1951, pp. 329-43.

Campbell, Joseph. *The Flight of the Wild Gander: Explorations in the Mythological Dimension.* New York: Viking Press, 1969.

_____. *The Hero with a Thousand Faces.* 2nd ed. Princeton: Princeton University Press, 1969.

_____. *The Mythic Image.* Princeton: Princeton University Press, 1974.

Chesler, Phyllis. *Women and Madness.* Garden City, N.Y.: Doubleday & Company, 1972.

Chodorow, Nancy. "Family Structure and Feminine Personality." In *Woman, Culture, and Society.* Ed. Michelle Zimbalist Rosaldo and Louise Lamphere. Stanford, Calif.: Stanford University Press, 1974, pp. 43-66.

_____. "Being and Doing: A Cross-Cultural Examination of the Socialization of Males and Females." In *Woman in Sexist Society.* Ed. Vivian Gornick and Barbara K. Moran. New York and London: Basic Books, 1971, pp. 173-97.

Cohen, Mabel Blake. "Personal Identity and Sexual Identity." *Psychiatry,* 29 (1966), 1-14.

Dinnerstein, Dorothy. *The Mermaid and the Minotaur: Sexual Arrangements and Human Malaise.* New York: Harper & Row, 1976.

Douglas, Wallace W. "The Meaning of 'Myth' in Modern Criticism." *Modern Philology,* 50 (1953), 232-42.

Edel, Leon. "D.R., 1882-1957." *Modern Fiction Studies,* 4 (1958), 165-68.

Eichner, Hans. "The Eternal Feminine: An Aspect of Goethe's Ethics." *Transactions of the Royal Society of Canada,* IV, 9 (1971), 235-44. Rpt. in *Faust: A Tragedy.* Trans. Walter Arndt. Ed. Cyrus Hamlin. New York: W.W. Norton, 1976, pp. 615-24.

Ellmann, Mary. *Thinking About Women.* New York: Harcourt, Brace & World, 1968.

Firestone, Shulamith. *The Dialectic of Sex: The Case for Feminist Revolution.* New York: Wm. Morrow, 1970.

Frye, Northrop. *Anatomy of Criticism: Four Essays.* Princeton: Princeton University Press, 1957.

_____. "The Archetypes of Literature." *Kenyon Review,* 13 (1951), 92-110.

Gillespie, Diane Filby. "Female Artists as Characters and Creators: The Dual Concern with Feminine Role and Feminine Fiction in the work of May Sinclair, Dorothy Richardson, and Virginia Woolf." Diss. Univ. of Alberta, 1974.

Goldberg, Gerald Jay. "The Artist-Novel in Transition." *English Fiction in Transition*, 4 (1961), 12-27.

Hamilton, Edith. *Mythology: Timeless Tales of Gods and Heroes*. New York: New American Library, 1940, 1942, 1969.

Heller, Erich. *The Artist's Journey into the Interior and Other Essays*. New York: Random House, 1965.

Holt, Robert. R. "The Development of Primary Process: A Structural View." In *Motives and Thought: Psychoanalytic Essays in Honor of David Rapaport*. Ed. Robert R. Holt. New York: International Universities Press, 1967, pp. 345-83.

Horney, Karen. "The Flight from Womanhood." *The International Journal of Psycho-Analysis*, 7 (1926), 324-39. Rpt. in *Psychoanalysis and Women: Contributions to New Theory and Therapy*. Ed. Jean Baker Miller, M.D. New York: Brunner/Mazel, 1973, pp. 3-16.

Janeway, Elizabeth. *Man's World, Woman's Place: A Study in Social Mythology*. New York: Wm. Morrow, 1971.

Jong, Erica. "Writer who 'flew' to sexy fame talks about being a woman." *Vogue*, March 1977, pp. 158-60.

Kerényi, C. *Eleusis: Archetypal Image of Mother and Daughter*. Trans. Ralph Manheim. Bollingen, 65, 4. New York: Pantheon Books, 1967.

Killoh, Ellen Peck. "The Woman Writer and the Element of Destruction." *College English*, 34 (October 1972), 31-38.

Kris, Ernst. *Psychoanalytic Explorations in Art*. New York: International Universities Press, 1952.

Lévi-Strauss, Claude. "The Structural Study of Myth." In *Myth: A Symposium*. Ed. Thomas A. Sebeok. Philadelphia: American Folklore Society, 1955, pp. 50-66.

Linton, Ralph. *The Cultural Background of Personality*. New York: Appleton-Crofts, 1945.

Malinowski, Bronislaw. *Myth in Primitive Psychology*. New York: W.W. Norton, 1926.

Marder, Herbert. *Feminism and Art: A Study of Virginia Woolf*. Chicago and London: University of Chicago Press, 1968.

Marmor, Judd. "Changing Patterns of Femininity." In *The Marriage Relationship.* Ed. Salo Rosenbaum and Ian Alger. New York: Basic Books, 1968. Rpt. in *Psychoanalysis and Women: Contributions to New Theory and Therapy.* Ed. Jean Baker Miller, M.D. New York: Brunner/Mazel, 1973, pp. 191-206.

May, Rollo. "The Daimonic in Psychotherapy." In *Love and Will.* New York: W.W. Norton, 1969, pp. 131-34.

Moers, Ellen. *Literary Women: The Great Writers.* Garden City, N.Y.: Anchor-Doubleday, 1977.

Neumann, Erich. *The Great Mother: An Analysis of the Archetype.* Trans. Ralph Manheim. Bollingen, 7. Princeton: Princeton University Press, 1955; rpt. 1974.

Nin, Anaïs. "On Feminism and Creation." *Michigan Quarterly Review,* 13 (1974), 4-13.

Ozick, Cynthia. "Women and Creativity: The Demise of the Dancing Dog." In *Woman in Sexist Society.* Ed. Vivian Gornick and Barbara K. Moran. New York and London: Basic Books, 1971, pp. 307-22.

Pannill, Linda. "The Artist-Heroine in American Fiction. 1890-1920." Diss. Univ. of N.C., Chapel Hill, 1975.

Pearson, Carol, and Katherine Pope, eds. *Who Am I This Time?":
Female Portraits in British and American Literature.* New York: McGraw-Hill, 1976.

Proudfit, Sharon Wood. "Lily Briscoe's Painting: A Key to Personal Relations in *To the Lighthouse.*" *Criticism,* 13 (Winter 1971), 26-39.

Rank, Otto. "The Myth of the Birth of the Hero." Trans. F. Robbins and Smith Ely Jelliffe. In *The Myth of the Birth of the Hero and Other Writings.* 1914; rpt. New York: Vintage Books, 1964, 1-96.

Rich, Adrienne. *Of Woman Born: Motherhood as Experience and Institution.* New York: W.W. Norton, 1976.

Rosaldo, Michelle Zimbalist. "Woman, Culture, and Society: A Theoretical Overview." In *Woman, Culture and Society.* Ed. Michelle Zimbalist Rosaldo and Louise Lamphere. Stanford, Calif.: Stanford University Press, 1974, pp. 17-42.

Salzman, Leon. "Psychology of the Female: A New Look." *Archives of General Psychiatry,* 17 (August 1967), 195-203. Rpt. in *Psychoanalysis and Women: Contributions to New Theory and Therapy.* Ed. Jean Baker Miller, M.D. New York: Brunner/Mazel, 1973, pp. 173-89.

Seidenberg, Robert. "Is Anatomy Destiny?" In *Marriage in Life and Literature*. New York: Philosophical Library, 1970, pp. 119-56.

Shroder, Maurice Z. *Icarus: The Image of the Artist in French Romanticism*. Cambridge: Harvard University Press, 1961.

Slater, Philip E. "Toward a Dualistic Theory of Identification." *Merrill-Palmer Quarterly of Behavior and Development*, 7 (April 1961), 113-26.

Spacks, Patricia Ann Meyer. *The Female Imagination*. New York: Random House, 1971.

Watts, Alan W. *Myth and Ritual in Christianity*. London: Thames, 1954.

Weinstein, Fred, and Gerald M. Platt. *Psychoanalytic Sociology: An Essay on the Interpretation of Historical Data and the Phenomena of Collective Behavior*. Baltimore and London: The Johns Hopkins University Press, 1973.

Wheelwright, Philip. "Notes on Mythopoeia." *Sewanee Review*, 59 (1951), 574-92.

_____. "The Semantic Approach to Myth." In *Myth: A Symposium*. Ed. Thomas A. Sebeok. Philadelphia: American Folklore Society, 1955, pp. 95-103.

Woolf, Virginia. *A Room of One's Own*. New York: Harcourt, Brace & World, 1929; rpt. New York: Harcourt, Brace, 1957.